A LIFE LIVED
ON THE UGLY BENCH

NICI SWAN

ISBN: 978-1-5272-6080-1

Disclaimer:

I have tried to recreate events, locales and conversations
from my memories of them. In order to maintain their
anonymity in some instances I have changed the names
of individuals and places. I may have also changed some
identifying characteristics and details such as physical
properties, occupations and places of residence.

Cover illustration: Emma Sally

WHY DID I WRITE THIS BOOK?

I look at the pictures of my great grandparents and wonder what their lives and their families were like and so I've written this for my own great grandchildren who I hope have the same curiosity as me, not that I'm anywhere near having any grandchildren at all at the moment. And my sister apparently says to my mother when she has tried to reconcile our family, which is rare: '*you don't know the half of it*'. I have asked her what this '*half of it*' is but she won't engage with me; so here it is, my '*half of it*'.

Also, I used to give talks in schools on food, alcohol, drugs (prescribed and not) and how they are all things that we use to fix ourselves. They were really well received, so well received they are another reason I wanted to write this all down. During these talks I would tell this story, the PG version, and a boy Nadia worked with recognised me and said to her, "that's it, I never listened to anyone at school but I listened to your Mum," bless you Cal.

It's been very emotional writing it, I pondered a few times on whether to finish it as it was SO painful. It evoked too many very difficult memories but in the words of Shrek, '*Better out than in*', and eventually it's proved enormously cathartic and I feel like a boulder of shame has been lifted from me.

It's not a pretty story but it is an honest one, you might form an opinion of me but one of the most crucial things I have learned in this little life of mine is that your problem with me is not my problem. The only opinion of me that matters is my own.

The title was difficult, others that were considered were '*Whore*', '*Slaaaag*', '*Warts 'n' all*', '*Wash hands after reading*' but I always came back to the one that haunted me and so it is. All aboard the rollercoaster, strap yourself in, it might be a bumpy ride.

I hope you smile, I think you'll cringe, I hope you enjoy.

·

Great grandparents Smith

Great grandparents Swan and family

CONTENTS

FAMILY AND BEFORE

Dad was born in 1934 and grew up in a workers' cottage on Dark Lane in Upper Castle Combe. He was third of four boys to Nan and Gramp and definitely the most handsome with beautiful cheekbones, fair hair and a gorgeous smile. Just stunning and he was always kind and caring. He met Mum on his milk round in Grittleton. Later at a dance, drunk, he said to his friend, "I'm gonna marry her," to which his friend replied, "don't be daft, she's posh".

During the war, as a small child from the garden, he saw the sky light up bright red with the bombs dropping over Bath and Bristol. He would watch the prisoners being marched from their barracks, where the circuit is now and they worked as farm labourers, along Upper Castle Combe every evening to the village hall on what is now White-gates, the estate at the top of Combe, for their dinner.

Aged seven or so he had to climb the church spire to wind the clock daily, but there was no clock face. It wasn't needed because most couldn't tell the time as they were agricultural workers. The clock was for the bell to ring for lunchtime. It does have one of the oldest working mechanisms in the country and you can pay 20p to see it in action still. There's also a crusader who fought in two crusades in the church, denoted by his legs being crossed.

My great grandparents are in the graveyard, and my Nan and Gramp are in the most idyllic spot where all are you can hear is the stream and trees rustling, where my ashes will be scattered one day, as far away from my mother as possible. I love the place, I still walk Eric, our dog, there sometimes. I only wish I were rich enough to live there but it's all owned by the Manor House Hotel and wealthy people now. They mostly turn up for weekends or holidays or even less than that, no villagers left at all. Breaks my Dad's heart. It feels like a ghost village to me but always beautiful and a hit for tourists. It was voted the prettiest village in England for years by the Americans because it was the village used in the original Dr Dolittle movie and has been used in many others since, including War Horse.

Nan and Gramp's cottage was owned by the dairy farmers who Gramp worked for. Every day Grampy would walk home with a grey metal jug of warm milk. I loved the cottage on Dark Lane, and in summer Claire and I would stay. Sometimes we'd walk over the field, through the sty and down into the village to meet friends, all children of people Dad had grown up with who he drank and played darts and cricket with who still lived mostly on Whitegates. Mum had stopped him playing football though because if he got injured how would they pay the mortgage?

Dad and his three brothers had all worked for the dairy at some point, Michael and Jonathon did so all their lives until they retired but Dad and Richard left. Richard, 'R Nipper', the youngest, was now an insurance salesman, the most financially successful of them, married with a daughter, a couple of years younger than me. Richard would read the *'hatched, matched and dispatched'* (births, marriages and deaths) every week in the Gazette and Herald and then go knocking on those doors to sell life insurance he told me.

Michael was married to Elaine, they never had children so Claire and I would stay there too, on the other side of the road in Upper Combe. Nan and Gramp owned their home which had once been a village shop. It had a well in the yard out the back with a huge slab of stone over it but there was just enough room to drop things and hear them splash. Elaine had an egg round that delivered to all the enormous farms and houses around and we loved going with her when we stayed.

Dad completed his conscription in the Army where he learned to drive heavy goods vehicles. He lodged in Birmingham at the time with a lady called Joan and her family. The daughter had a boyfriend who was a musician, later they formed a band and had a No1 with '*Keep on Running*'. The boyfriend, Muff, became the Chairman of CBS records and Elton John is the godfather to their daughter who a few years ago, I saw, got a job as Deputy Fashion Editor at The Independent when she left Uni. His brother is quite famous even now, Whitney's '*Higher Love*' is his. Zena, the daughter, was one of Mum and Dad's bridesmaids, but oddly I have no clue about the other bridesmaid. It's a very tenuous claim to fame my mother loves to hang on to, perhaps I do too.

Dad had a lot of relatives, no doubt because his parents both had eight or nine brothers and sisters. He had Aunts that lived along Summer Lane in a big house with Uncle Simon who smoked a pipe that stank, just like Grampy's, and they had a dog racing track out front and lots of Irishmen would turn up with greyhounds to race from time to time. These Aunts were the ones who would utter 'she did well, considerin' whenever they mentioned Nan. Kindly women though, Aunty Nell and Aunty Nan, who later moved to the big house halfway down the hill to Combe in a house swap. There was a back yard and then a sheer drop above from a field and sometimes a cow would wander too far and plunge to its death. There was another relative who was a baker and we'd stop in the bakery with Aunty Elaine when we went to the village and get fresh baked bread.

My lovely Nan would make sugar sandwiches from a fresh cottage loaf that she'd cradle in her arm and slice so thinly you could see through it, she'd butter it and sprinkle it with the white stuff, sublime. She amassed a whole larder of sugar in the 70s when it was reported that there may be a shortage so every Friday when her and Aunty Elaine came to town to do their weekly shop at Greggs, she'd buy two or three 2lb bags. I can see her larder now, stacked from the floor to the ceiling with bags of sugar. Nan also made the BEST mashed potato, with loads of butter and the cream from the top of the milk. Whenever we stayed there we would have supper, such a treat to have supper, usually cold meat, bread and butter and pickle or something similar.

Mum's Mum, owned the village stores in Grittleton where they'd moved to from Melksham. Mum and her two sisters did all the work in the shop though. They'd lost their Dad to high blood pressure when Mum was fourteen, there isn't a photo of him without a cigarette in his hand. Mum started smoking at eleven and would sit in the bathroom on the loo with her head hanging out of the window to smoke.

Mum had two sisters, Sylvia the eldest married to Stephen, a stockman in Kington St Michael, they lived in a tied house and had three boys, all similar ages to us. Their house had an odd smell, not dirty, just odd, I always thought it was the parquet flooring, but I don't know. All I remember about visiting them was that Aunty Sylvia used to shout what seemed like constantly, 'bloody kids'. She had enormous breasts and spina bifida which meant she had very tiny feet with an incredibly high instep and a hole in the bottom of her spine apparently that I didn't know anything about. Stephen was a lovely gentle soul and Sylvia was always kind too, she didn't like her mum much, not sure why but I can guess, she wasn't a particularly nice woman as I recall either.

Judy, Mum's middle sister, was married to Bernie, a painter and decorator and she was now a top boss's secretary. They had three children, also similar ages to us and they lived in Chippenham in a three bed semi with Nan in the sitting room because she'd given them some money to buy their first home when she'd sold the shop in Grittleton. It was well known that Mum's Mum's favourite grandchild was Judy and Bernie's daughter because she'd seen her born at home. She never seemed to move from her chair, I rarely recall seeing her out of it.

We used to go on holidays with Judy and Bernie staying in small bed and breakfast places in Bournemouth, Helston and Newquay. We loved Newquay and Lusty Glaze beach where we'd hire a beach hut. Mum and

Judy would make cheese and tomato or ham rolls for lunch and drinks from this hut. Dad and Bernie would play space tennis while the tide was out, and they'd hit the ball so high I thought it'd never come out of the clouds. I loved it when the tide came in and we'd body surf in on the waves, absolutely loved it, still love boogie boarding.

EVERYBODY HATES YOU!

Mum and Dad married when they were twenty and twenty-five and rented two rooms in Church Cottage opposite the shop in Grittleton, where I was conceived. I was born on 12th September 1962 in Greenways, the maternity hospital, and we lived in Grittleton until I was two.

They bought their first home on Cherry Tree Crescent in Chippenham, or Honeymoon Alley as it was apparently nicknamed because all the residents were young couples with small children.

Two years later along came my sister Claire. Three years later Kerry was born and I can vaguely recall being given a Tiny Tears doll when we visited Greenways.

Dad always worked away from Monday to Friday, leaving before we woke up on a Monday and coming home at teatime on a Friday, his nights out/away money was needed and long-distance driving was what he liked doing.

From very early on I was always very aware that Mum liked Claire and Kerry but wasn't quite so fond of me, I was bright but downtrodden. I never felt good enough or that I fitted in. I always felt left out and Mum would often assure me of as much when she was angry, which was quite often when Dad was away, pointing her finger in my face and yelling, "everybody hates you and it's all your fault" and, "why don't you listen, why don't you ever get anything right?" and, "don't you ever lie". I couldn't figure out what was my fault though and why everybody hated me, but I was sure they did. I would get upset at these remarks and she would say angrily, "you shouldn't feel like that, why do you feel like that?" asking the question but not wanting the answer. To defend myself, I'd get angry to make myself seem big and strong and powerful because I thought that then they'd be scared of me and wouldn't hurt me anymore. Rather like the Gruffalo and the mouse scenario. But she'd ridicule me with one of her favourite put downs, "you've got the Swan temper, you're just like your father". Claire soon realised how painful these words were to me and copied them.

Claire was very popular, in the crescent and at school, with fair skin, blue eyes and long blonde hair and Mum told everyone she was, "the pretty and clever one" so, with my self-worth low anyway, I concluded I must be ugly and thick. I was taller than most, so, "bigger boned," Mum would say, with brown hair, freckles, green eyes, NHS horn-rimmed glasses, when I dared to wear them, and slightly large front teeth. My hair had been long but a neighbour's son painted it with blue gloss paint and Mum cut it all short and she was no hairdresser.

Friends of Mum and Dad's would remark how much I looked like Dad which didn't seem like a compliment as a little girl, especially when he sometimes had a beard. I always wanted to be the pretty one in the zodiac *please let me be the pretty one sometime* I would wish constantly.

Mum would take Claire and me to town, me running beside the pushchair, trying to keep up, and if my hand let go she would shout at me. Seeing Nan Swan on the other side of the high street one Friday I ran across to her embrace. Mum followed and scolded me so hard a passer-by stopped and told her she should be reported to Social Services.

In the evenings Mum would curl up on the sofa with Claire on one side and Kerry on the other and read stories while I sat alone in the single armchair opposite longing to be cuddled like that. I remember vividly standing in the kitchen doorway watching as Mum played with Claire on one side of the draining board and Kerry on the other while they washed up, all laughing and smiling, always wondering why I wasn't allowed to sit up there too.

Dad would return on Friday evenings and the arguing would ensue. We spent our childhood around village pubs at weekends while Mum and Dad socialised and played darts. When the drink drive laws came in they'd decided Dad would continue to drink, and Mum would continue to smoke, so she could drive him, he needed his license obviously.

On Sunday's in summer we'd spend hours and hours at cricket, mostly in Grittleton as Dad played for the Neeld Arms. There would be other children of the cricketers to while away the long, long hours with. There was a very high swing and a slide we'd play on at the bottom of the cricket field and sometimes we'd walk through the woods behind the cricket pavilion until we got scared and ran back. The highlight was going back to the Neeld afterwards and having a bottle of coke and a packet of golden wonder crisps with a pickled egg in, what a treat that was.

I liked primary school, but was regularly told off for being bossy, it's mentioned in all my school reports, a word I loathe to this day, a word that terrified me throughout all my school years. And I was always so much bigger than almost everyone else, taller really, but I felt that must be what made me fat, and therefore ugly. I was always the forfeit in kiss chase and Claire was always the prize, along with Heather and Susan, the two girls I called my friends. They were beautiful too, both blonde, both pretty, all the boys wanted to be their boyfriends, but never mine.

I was also friends with Sally and one day, aged six or so, I persuaded her to run away with me, not sure why but I must've been hurting over something. So we walked along Biddestone Lane almost as far as the brook where the fossils are found, but we got scared and decided to go back. When we got home to Sally's both mums were furious, but no-one ever asked why we'd done it that I recall.

There was a fashion design competition at school and foolishly I must've asked or let Gill, our neighbour, draw something for me and it won. When they asked me to do something else I couldn't, and the shame of cheating left a heavy wound. I don't know why I cheated, just wish I hadn't. Perhaps I just wanted to be good at something for a change.

I was bullied by a girl at primary school, Dad worked with her Dad and we used to visit them sometimes, she would secretly punch and kick me for no reason. No idea why.

Mr Frost, when I was nine and the first to wear a bra in my class, used to ping my bra strap when he walked behind my chair. And Mr Harris removed me from the class at the end of a day when he'd asked everyone to put their chairs on the table and they didn't. I went around doing it for them so he proceeded to drag me outside the classroom and told me off which I really couldn't understand because I was only doing what he'd asked that other people weren't doing?

The controlling behaviour was setting in, I had to try and do every-thing for everyone because then perhaps they might like me. Or maybe it was because I thought no-one could do it as well as I could, so I'd rather do it myself to make sure it was right, I'm really not sure, I've never forgotten it though.

I walked to school with Claire usually. We'd stop at the shop on the corner of the busy road and with 10p I'd buy an apple pie, a packet of crisps and an apple, may have been a sweet too, and that was my lunch. One day I was alone, walking to school and rather than walk to the lollipop lady to cross I crossed on my own before reaching her and it's a really busy road. That morning in assembly this dreadful deed was mentioned and I felt all the staff staring at me, I have no idea why I did it but I suspect I was craving attention and there's no such thing as bad attention, like there's no such thing as bad publicity, ask Hugh Grant.

To a child being told off is attention, and when you rarely get any, it'll do. No doubt this act of defiance was my way of screaming for help as I couldn't make sense of what was going on at home, all the screaming and shouting, all the tears from Mum all week and all I could do was hug her legs and yet she'd push me away and cuddle Claire and Kerry sobbing after another phone call with Dad. And he would come home on Friday and she'd be SO nice to him like nothing had happened. She'd tread on eggshells around him and smother him with love and I never got any, ever, bar when I went to Nan Swans where she would welcome me with outstretched arms longing to hold me and hug me. I loved being at Nan Swan's.

There were a lot of children on Cherry Tree Crescent and we all played together generally, although I never felt like anyone really wanted me to play but I did join in if they let me.

The detached house opposite was sold and a removal van arrived with a blonde boy looking out of the window. I swooned, I must have been seven or eight. Our house was only a semi so they were posh.

The boy was Philip and his mother and father ran a local shop in town. They had Fiesta (soft porn) magazines under their bed which we used to thumb through when they weren't around. One day, aged about aged eight or nine, John, the father, walked in Philip's bedroom and there I was, with my pants off, bum in the air, copying a pose from Fiesta, with Philip drawing me, so even then I was going rather overboard to try and get a boy to like me. It was also Philip who I tried my first cigarette with, coupying down behind a hedge on a playing field while the traffic roared along the busy road. I didn't like it at all, made me cough horrendously and besides I already had something to fix me much more accessible and acceptable, the white stuff, sugar, which I'd spoon directly from the bowl, often.

Playgroup, I'm 2nd left bottom row, the boy on my right was the one who painted my hair with blue gloss.

WHAT'S WRONG WITH ME?

I remember sitting with Philip in the single armchair watching the moon landing, or was it the return to earth? and I would sit in that same armchair watching Mum cuddle Claire and Kerry while my heart pained so I'd have another spoon or three of sugar, but I SO wanted to be loved by Mum and Dad, and a boy. Claire was always loved by everyone and yet no-one ever even liked me, what was wrong with me?

Further down Cherry Tree Crescent, opposite, were Bryony and Susan and their Mum Celia. Celia used to have parties, it's been rumoured some were keys in the bowl parties but I can't confirm. Mum was friendliest with Diane, Cath (Philips mum opposite) and Celia.

Celia had a party in about '71 and Claire and I slept in the attic with Bryony and Susan and a lot of practice kissing ensued, that's how we learn to kiss isn't it? By practising on friends?

At this party Mum danced with Brian who was single and lived next door to Celia and world war three erupted in our house afterwards. Late one night soon after I woke up so walked into Mum and Dad's bedroom to find Dad straddling Mum with his hands around her throat and was told to go back to bed, everything was alright. Eventually Mum kicked Dad out and he moved back to Nans. I was relieved; at least we were getting rid of the man that made Mum cry so much. All I was interested in was the fact that I'd get two Christmas and birthday presents, seemed like a good idea to me. That Christmas Dad picked us up and drove us to Nans crying all the way, declaring his love for us all. It was a beautiful frosty, sunny Christmas day and all we did was cry the whole journey. Pete Skellerns 'You're a lady' always reminds me of this time.

Dad came to collect us one day and I remember Mum holding a hot iron up to ward him off while he was crying telling her how much he loved her, after all her tears and heartache and pain. I just couldn't understand it, I could give her all that love, why did she need him? She soon had him back and I walked in the bathroom sometime later after being woken up to find them having a bath together, laughing raucously, all was fine, just fine, until the next time.

Mum did put me in clubs, I did ballet, brownies and guides at various times. Our first club was Sunday School at the Chapel in Upper Combe. I liked going because Claire and I got dressed up in these gorgeous pink pleated skirts with matching jackets. I liked 'The Illustrated Children's Bible' and the stories in it but spent most of the time looking at the pictures, I'm not a lover of reading. When I did my family tree around 2012 I discovered that Gramp's family had moved from London to Bath to work at Widcombe Baptist Church. Then they moved out to Castle Combe to work as preachers at the Chapel. Dad could recite the bible, not that he ever did but when Boney M released '*By the rivers of Babylon*' he instantly said, "that's in the bible". We were all surprised as we had no idea of his religious upbringing, but Nan was the daughter of a gypsy I later learned so no doubt his upbringing was quite religious. Whenever we stayed there Nan would always make us kneel and pray before we got into bed and we'd, "thank the Lord for what we about to receive," whenever we ate there. And Dad's Aunt Dot who lived at Kent's Bottom taught at the Sunday school.

My two favourite clubs were The Dazzlers and the local swimming club.

Mum must've joined me in The Dazzlers when I was eight or nine, they were a singing and dancing troupe who put on pantomines and shows in the Neeld Hall most, if not every year. There were different age groups from four/five, I think, then us, then the older girls and then some adults, but there were a lot of us. It was all run by Will and Cleo, he played piano and they tweaked songs to get around copyright and she tirelessly taught dance routines. We'd spend an hour a week, in halls practising routines, learning steps and songs and when the next show was announced it was more hours, but we loved it. All the costumes were made, and I think paid for, by us. We spent hours making pom, poms, garlands and heavens knows what else. I have many photos done by a professional, again if I recall, possibly Will, of me as a cat, a kite, a dwarf, a flowerpot and heavens knows what else. The Dazzlers were a huge thing for everyone involved and they were quite good, the adults were good enough to get a week at the Theatre Royal in Bath for their 'Black and White Minstrel Show', keep that quiet now though.

My very favourite club was the swimming club which I joined at nine or so. We had the most fabulous Olympic 50m outdoor pool in Chippenham, so it was only open from April/May to September. I loved it because I could do it and was fairly good at it, better than Claire who wasn't into it at all. When it closed through winter we went all over the place for training, Corsham, Colerne, Calne and again for at least an hour a week, more in summer when Chippenham was open. My primary school had a small 10m above-ground pool too so I got to swim there as well but not often.

Around this time I was becoming constipated a lot, I now know this was because of the sugar I was consuming, spooning it from the bowl at every opportunity especially when I was hurting, when Claire and Kerry would be loved by Mum and I'd be rejected and loathed and blamed constantly for anything and everything. I was often at the doctors with a hard tummy and he'd prescribe laxatives in the form of granules that were aniseed which I didn't like, I still don't like liquorice, fennel or aniseed and never drank Pernod or Ouzo.

I used to bite my nails badly too, and would rip the skin on and around my nails which would give me whitlows that I'd squeeze until I could bear the pain no longer and they'd burst and the puss would come out. A very primitive form of self-harm for a six/seven-year-old which continued well into my teens, in fact I didn't stop biting my nails until I was eighteen.

Our neighbour sorted the situation with Brian from down the road when he asked him if he wanted to take on Mum and three children, which he didn't. By June of '72 we'd moved to Hythe in Hampshire because it was near another depot that Dad could work from in Fawley, and away from Brian. I was glad to be moving, no-one would know me, no-one would know that everybody hated me, or that it was all my fault, I could start fresh, from a clean page. Thank goodness for that.

We sold our house in Cherry Tree Crescent to Aunty Nancy and Uncle Jonathon, she still lives there today. Isn't it odd how when you now visit old childhood memories the street seems so small and yet as a child it seemed to take ages to walk along it and the house seems tiny too.

HOPE

So we moved to Hollybank Road in Hythe to a bungalow in May of '72. Mum and Dad bought it from a circus family and it stank and was flea infested and our back garden was three feet higher than our neighbours as every time the weeds grew they'd have more top soil delivered. It was big compared to Cherry Tree Crescent though and needed decorating from top to bottom.

We all enrolled at the local primary school and on my first day my new teacher sat me at the front next to Gary because I could, "sort 'im out". He was the son of the local record shop owner. I liked Gary immediately, he was chatty, loud, olive skinned with buck teeth and he had a love of all things pop, as did I. So much so that I would rush home, a ten-minute sprint, every Tuesday lunchtime to write down the Top 20 as delivered by Johnny Walker on Radio 1. There was always massive excitement on my return, especially when Gary Glitters '*Leader of the Gang*' (or was it '*I love you love*'?) went straight to No 1.

Claire became very good friends with Karen down the road, Julie two doors up and Sherry up the hill, all these girls were my age but Claire was their friend. I always thought no one ever wanted me as a friend because I wasn't pretty and Claire was, and that record still played in my mind (everybody hates you...).

There was a girl at primary school who was a friend, she was tall and big boned like me and when we went to secondary school one day we were sitting on the field and she had her head in my lap and some boys walked passed and called out, "lezzies", did they really think I was a lesbian? I'd always been in love with so many boys?

It was probably the first time I'd thought about it but I was questioning my sexuality at this time. I used to look at my genitals and think maybe that's going to become a willy, this went on for years, literally years, until I started periods I suspect, wondering if I was really a boy, but was I gay? That stayed with me until my twenties, or possibly later, not because I was attracted to women but because I never had boyfriends.

Every week we were in Hythe Mum received the Wiltshire Gazette and Herald which Judy, her sister would send, to keep up on the gossip and news. We'd return to Chippenham very regularly and we'd have people visit quite often too. Mum never let go of where we came from. I loved living in Hythe because nobody knew me, no one knew I was thick, fat, ugly, horrible, bossy, I felt that I'd left all of that behind. And I did, it got a bit better, so much so I didn't want to leave.

There wasn't quite so much screaming and shouting between Mum and Dad in Hythe either but I do recall Kerry having a bed wetting problem and so a rubber cover was fitted under the sheet on her bed and if water touched it a very loud bell would ring. One night this bell went off and I remember Dad pulling her out of her bed by her arm and spanking her violently while she sobbed, as did we, screaming, "stop it, stop it Dad, stop it". It sent shivers down me, the memory still does.

Julie up the road had an older sister, Moira who had some weighing scales and was always talking about her weight and I started to weigh myself there every day after school. I'd be 8'10, 8'12, 8'13, yo-yoing up and down, at ten years old, and I started to restrict my food, and then binge biscuits or cake, if only I could be small, like Claire, perhaps then people would like me. I started to exercise excessively in my bedroom, doing lots of sit-ups and jumping jacks, and collapsed. The doctor was called, all was well.

My bedroom had bright orange walls, not that you could see them because they were completely covered with posters of Donny and The Osmonds. Claire's bedroom, which was the biggest, always, was purple and adorned with pictures of David Cassidy and The Bay City Rollers. We'd spend hours trying to perfect Osmonds dance routines with Joanna from over the road and I'd try to play the tunes on a piano we had for a while, the best I ever got though was chopsticks very badly. 70s pop is still my favourite era and I love listening to Johnny on a Sunday without fail, though usually on Sounds, can be a bit too rock and not enough pop sometimes though.

Mum had a friend who we called Aunty but she wasn't. Aunty Jean who was the wife of Uncle Ron who'd been Dad's boss previously, but Dad had got the sack because he had an affair with the boss's wife, who was a bit of a one. I met someone recently who said the same of her, she'd tried it on with him as a teenager too. Jean and Ron had two daughters, Claire and Jade our ages. Claire suffered with asthma and consequently they were the first people we knew to have duvets rather than blankets, and acrylic carpets rather than wool. One Sunday morning we had a phone call from Uncle Ron to say Claire had collapsed and died, of asthma, it was horrifying and seems hardly believable now but back then it wasn't as controllable. A few weeks before I'd bought '*Claire*' by Gilbert O'Sullivan, I could never find it after that, thank goodness, still always reminds me of her and that time.

Once or twice on Saturday mornings Claire, Sherry, Karen and I got get dressed up in our best clothes, long skirts were favourites then, and we'd take the ferry over to Southampton to walk to the nightclub at the top of the High Street where they would have a Saturday Morning Disco. The boys would run around like mad things, we loved getting ready more than the disco I'm sure, but Claire, Sherry and Karen would always be asked to dance and I never was. I was always on the ugly bench.

I saw Stardust, because David Essex was SO hot. It was the first time I'd seen nudity, albeit part nudity, on a screen too. I went with Karen, feeling like a spare prick at a wedding while she snogged another boyfriend and I stood as look out.

Julie was massively into horse riding and we'd spend hours with hats on, (though my head was too big for one of hers' so I had to go without) and twigs as whips in our hand. Cantering around her garden, hands poised in reign holding position, jumping over boxes and branches, anything that could act as a fence, pretending we were in an equestrian ring. At weekends Julie would go to the local stables to work all day and once or twice I went too. Then, for my birthday I suspect, Mum and Dad paid for me to go for a proper ride, £5 for an hour's ride. They put me on the biggest horse, Astro, a shire or cobb, as I was too big to go on the dainty ponies, or that's what my head told me, but the owner of the stables confirmed it too. The hours ride felt like five minutes, I loved it, absolutely loved it, I couldn't ride but I could stay on.

There was an older boy over the road, Robert, who took Claire and I to see Slade in Southampton for my twelfth birthday because it was that wonderful glam rock time. We had seats in the front row of the circle and with everyone jumping up and down I could see the balcony moving and I was terrified it was going to collapse but it was my first ever concert and I loved it, and Slade. They came to Goldigger's around my twenty-second birthday so I saw them again, love their pop hits still.

We'd spend afternoons at Ippley River swinging on a rope over the river, having picnics when people visited, loved Ippley River. We went swimming at Southampton pool, it was close to the ferry, and a man approached Mum and asked me to race a boy and then he asked us to go to their training sessions so we did, but not for long that I recall, bit of a long way in a car on dark winter nights.

I still have letters from Heather and Susan who wrote to me while we lived in Hythe and one summer I stayed with Heather and her family who were now living in what seemed like a huge farmhouse at Patterdown, with an Aga, very posh. Heather was very into horses too, so I spent the week watching her riding and doing gymkhanas, me being too heavy to ride her pony. And her sister, she was stunning, so beautiful and they both had boyfriends, always.

UNLOVABLE

In June 74 we moved back to Chippenham, to Aylesbury Road which Mum and Dad bought for £12,250 and I went to the girls' school, no other choice. I walked into my new tutor room and there were Heather and Susan, it was like I'd never been away.

A few days later I met a girl called Caroline who was rather like me, 5'7" tall and a similar size, I was five pounds heavier, and she was in the swimming club. We became friends. Another girl remarked when she met me, "at least someone can hit Caroline back now". Perhaps I'd met my match?

Throughout those secondary school years we spent the summer at Chippenham outdoor pool on a £3.25 season ticket, arriving at 10am, waiting for the gates to open and leaving at 6pm almost every day, bar the ones it rained on probably. Everybody from school would be there, all day, and we'd do swimming club too.

I got my first job at eleven or twelve years old, actually Caroline and I both got the job, collecting Vernon's pools money for the Dad of a girl at the swimming club. He would sit in his car while we went door to door collecting the coupons and money they owed, we'd get £3 a night for about two or three hours work. It was OK on a sunny evening but when it was pouring with rain and a howling gale it wasn't much fun, but the people we met were always nice so I liked it.

We'd save the money and get the train to Bath to go to Chelsea Girl and buy matching outfits but in different colours so we could swap them when we went out. Now we were going to swimming galas and it was never really about the swimming, it was always about who was going to get off with who on the coach on the way back and again Caroline was the one with the boyfriend, never me. And Claire, Claire always had a boyfriend, always.

I did have a boyfriend once. Caroline and I met Paul and Rich, probably at the swimming pool and somehow Paul became my boyfriend, a lovely looking boy. It was only very short lived, they came to our house on their bikes one day on the way to school and I couldn't bear it, he had to go. Caroline continued to go out with Rich though.

We finished working for Vernon's pools and got jobs in The Bear Hotel in Chippenham on 25p per hour. I'd work Tuesday and Thursday evenings 6-9pm and Saturday mornings and sometimes Sundays, washing up and occasionally waitressing or as a chamber maid. The kitchen was above the public bar and you could hear the thud, thud of the juke box and I became rather good at 'name that tune in...'

Mr and Mrs Smith the owners of The Bear, had a daughter who had two small children and a very handsome husband, a bit Oliver Reed, and I would babysit for the children quite often but rarely took any money, just liked being alone, bar the sleeping children, in a different house, watching TV and writing a diary.

While we were working there the News of the World was a broad-sheet and one Sunday on pages two and three there was a huge double page spread with a picture of the hotel and an article all about how it was the drugs hub for the UK. The drugs would come down from London and be distributed from there all over the country. Not sure anyone ever got done for it though, years later it was a favourite drinking hole of the local constabulary.

Caroline's sister Alison worked there. I was developing at this time, aged twelve or thirteen, and Alison made a remark about my boobs being saggy, I was so hurt and humiliated I started wearing wired bras. I always had bigger breasts than other girls, and that Boxing Day I started my periods and spent the day rolling around on my bed in agony. I suffered badly with acne constantly and used to always have boils on my neck, in my armpits and on the backs of my knees. Mum would buy magnesium sulphate, put it on gauze and stick it over the boils to draw them out. I was at the doctors a lot, often asking how I could lose weight. He'd give me a sheet with a diet on which obviously never worked but I'd do it for a few days, starve myself as much as possible and then binge the cakes and biscuits I loved as usual.

At school every day we'd wait in the coach park between the girls and the boys school to meet our friends. I knew a lot of these people from the villages because I'd spent so much time there as a child. And there were village discos that we were now becoming old enough to get in to. Caroline and I would go all over the place, Yatton Keynell, Castle Combe, Biddestone, Burton, Acton Turville, Hullavington, Christian Malford, Sutton Benger to name a few. We'd put on our best clothes, from Chelsea Girl and Dad or Mum would drive us there and collect us, it was usually my parents that did the taxi service, rarely others.

The first one Caroline and I went to, aged twelve, was in Hullavington. I wore a very slim dark brown pencil skirt with a small slit up the back that I'd made, with a white shirt that I sprayed with starch to make the collar stand up. I rolled the sleeves up just above my wrists and wore a wide black waspy belt as tight as I could bear to give me a waist and black stilettos to make me tall, then I wouldn't look so fat. We went to the Queens Head pub and ordered port and lemon and got served with no problem at all. When we were at the disco we drank sweet cider as it was cheaper. At the end of the night when the smooches came on a boy asked me to dance and while we danced I asked how old he thought I was and he said, "twenty-one". I kept quiet.

The first Burton disco I went to a boy called Mick asked me to dance when the smooches came on and we danced to '*Dream, Dream, Dream*' by the Everley Brothers. He was tall and big built and mixed race with afro hair which wasn't the in thing. On the Monday the school bus arrived and he came over and gave me a letter, it said 'Dear Nicky, I love you very much...'and a whole page of adoration and I was SO embarrassed because nobody fancied Mick, he wasn't the one all the girls wanted, that was Greg, who Claire was going out with. So I ran a mile and low and behold a few months later he was top of the pops and everyone wanted to date him, including Claire and he went out with all of them. We did remain friends though. Some months, or was it years later, drunk, at another Burton disco I did snog him around the back of the chicken shed that the discos were in and I felt my first ever penis. I put my hand around it and oh my god they ain't all that size I discovered from thereon, unfortunately. Scared me beyond belief, almost shrieked and walked off as quickly as I could back to the crowd of people that had just left the disco.

For a while I was besotted with Oli, another boy from Burton, who had bright green eyes, it was often about the eyes, he was never interested in me though. One day he came over to me in the school coach park and said, in front of everyone, "I have never, and will never, be interested in you". Completely humiliated me in front of everyone I knew in the coach park. Boys always liked the other girls they never liked me, maybe that was because I didn't like me.

Dad was delivering Bristol cream sherry, and we'd always had a flagon of it on the side in the kitchen. We'd decant this sherry into bottles and take it to the discos and drink it before we went inside, because the object of the exercise was to get drunk and snog boys.

I'd started writing a diary when I was nine-ish, not daily but some-times, I've still got them. By this time I was writing a bit more regularly and at the back of this diary there was a table. It had the boy's name, then marks out of ten for looks, personality, dress and WHT. WHT? Wandering hand trouble, they got a high score if they didn't try and tit you up.

The girl's school was OK, I liked it. I was very aware that I was thick, and ugly, compared to Claire, as Mum had told people many times, and the fact that she had boyfriends and I never did confirmed it in my head. Claire began adding, "and you're unlovable and you never have boyfriends," to the, "everybody hates you and it's all your fault", just for good measure.

I was in the third set for everything apart from maths because I was quite good at arithmetic which I really liked, still do. I liked making clothes too, Miss Williams was my needlework teacher, she was nice and I liked her classes, and I liked cookery lessons with Miss Brookes. I loved baking and would often make cakes and scones. I'd eat them in small portions with my family and then in secret I'd binge them. I was bullied at secondary school though, by a girl from Audley Road, she'd walk past and knock up against me, no clue why.

Claire was in the top set for everything, she was clever, but when she left she got the same O level results as me, she didn't get any better and she'd been in the brainy sets? No doubt she was never cleverer than me, it was just my lovely mother telling me and everyone else that she was, but as children we don't have the ability to see that these grown-ups who we're learning everything from are sick and wrong, cruel and unkind. There's a reason why my mother had to put me down, why she was so insecure and had to blame someone else for her husband's affairs because obviously if she didn't blame someone else she'd have to look at herself and her relationship with Dad and their marriage. You wouldn't want to upset that applecart would you, far easier to blame a defenceless child for all your problems.

George, a boy from primary was still on my radar, I still fancied him, he was at the boy's school. I'd slap his arm to get his attention, just fling my arm out to the side and collide with his. At an Hullavington disco one time he was there and some Malmesbury boys were bored and wanted to cause trouble so I told them to beat him up. They didn't, that I know of, but I've always felt very guilty for having told them to do so, it was unkind and I loathe that in anyone. I apologised to his wife when I met her many, many years later on another night, she was totally unaware of the incident, obviously, but at least I'd apologised for my malice. At that time I would want to hurt people who hurt me, if you hurt me I'd want to hurt you twice as hard back, revenge I suppose, not a good trait, cruel.

I was also loud to get attention because I never felt I did and the bigger I got the less attention I received so the louder I became. Being big, to me, is like wearing black, I felt invisible, unseen, unheard, so I was loud and quite outrageous given the chance. And all I ever wanted was to be loved, but I never felt I was, apart from when I was at Nan's.

I swear it's why I've always had a love addiction problem. I always believed if I could get 'that boy' I'd be OK, I'd be saved, he could fix me, just being loved could fix me.

Once or twice we had parties with all our friends because Mum and Dad would usually go out to the pub on Friday and Saturday nights. They were quite large parties, we'd have eighty to a hundred people in our three-bed semi, there's photographic evidence. I always took the photographs because I couldn't bear being in them. And if we didn't have a party we'd have fifteen to twenty friends over to drink coffee and eat cake that I'd make hoping they wouldn't eat too much of it so I could eat the lot when they'd left. Mum was buying eight plus packets of biscuits a week and never questioning where they went. I would come home from school every day, make tea or coffee with two teaspoons of sugar and dunk a whole packet of rich tea, digestives or golden crunch in them and consume the whole packet in minutes.

Although we had all these friends around I believed deep down that everybody still didn't really like me, they liked Claire, she was always popular because she was so pretty, it was only because I was generous that they were my friends, I had to buy friends.

Because we lived ten minutes from school and some lessons were boring we'd skive off school, especially Wednesday mornings, four or five of us would register and then walk home until lunchtime when we'd return. We had RE (religious education), English and PE on that morning and Mrs Jefferies was glad we didn't go I'm sure. Sometimes the boys would join us and there would ten or fifteen of us at ours all skiving together, drinking copious amounts of instant coffee and listening to pop music on the record player.

O LEVELS

When it came to choosing subjects for our O Levels I wasn't allowed to opt for physics or geography because I wasn't clever enough I was told. My geography teacher was the headmaster, who just after we left school had a child with a sixth former. When we did our end of year exams both teachers read the results out backwards because I'd come top in both and yet they didn't think I was capable. I wonder if that's because of all the trouble at home, all the arguing, screaming and shouting and consequently I'd play up at school. I've since learned from teachers I know that they are very aware it's not the children that are the problem, children are only a reflection of their home life.

On one occasion Mrs Jefferies, our head of year came barging into our classroom where Caroline and I were sitting at the front and shouted, "it was you two wasn't it," and we both said, "yes," and yet we had no clue what she was talking about but were just dumbstruck, and it wasn't us at all. I always took the blame for everything. I'd learned everything was always my fault.

I'd faint at school, used to starve myself and then collapse and I ran out of classes in tears a few times because of the crap that was going on at home. I don't know that I was naughty but I know I was screaming for attention because I felt I never got any, or perhaps that was love.

Everybody had boyfriends, Claire especially, everybody bar me, or so I thought. All my schoolbooks were adorned with 'so and so for me', 'I love ...', I still have them. One day I went into Mum and Dad's bedroom and there was a list on their shelf with options if I didn't change my behaviour. The last one was Grittleton House School which astounded me because I don't really think I was the problem, I was just a reaction to what was going on in their marriage, which was a complete nightmare, and there was absolutely no way they would ever have afforded to put me at a private school, ever.

We'd never been to London as a family, or at all that I know of, so after a lot of persuasion Dad said he'd take us. We all got dressed up and he drove us to London, and we saw all the industrial estates. We cried with laughter. We wanted to see the sights but all he knew were the industrial estates and he took us to a horrible pub for lunch which we also found hilarious. He did see the funny side too though, eventually. We did laugh a lot sometimes, why do I struggle to remember those times? Is it my defence mechanism, do I recall the bad rather than the good to keep me safe from it happening again? Possibly I suppose.

Mum was working at an estate agents and auctioneers and on a Friday, at the cattle market she would book in the pigs, her very favourite job. She knew and loved all the farmers and believed they were wealthy often confirming this belief with, "you'll never see a farmer on a bike". She worked with a man called Henry who she really had the hots for and often mentioned. He was quite posh. I later learned she'd been seen holding his hand under a table but I'm not sure she had an affair with him. Dad loathed him, I know that much.

While I was at the girls' school we had a letter home about bullying. It transpired that one of the girls had a journalist parent and so part of our letter ended up on Page 3 in the Sun, next to the boobs, and the school was rather embarrassed.

When choosing O level options I was keen on being a chef, then a dietician, trying to figure out why I couldn't stop eating, although at that age I was quite fit because I played hockey and was fairly active with swimming too. I also thought about becoming a physiotherapist but that's as far as it got. Towards the end of the fifth year (year eleven now) at the girl's school we all had a careers interview with our parents, or parent. The Careers Advisor, a little ginger, Scottish lady whose name I can't recall, spoke to us for about two minutes and then said, "you'll be married with children by the time you're nineteen, don't worry about it", and that was it, end of careers advice. All the girls at school wanted to get married and have children, but I never did, I just couldn't understand why they'd want to do that, or more importantly, why I didn't want to do that.

Around this time at a village disco I met a boy called Niall who used to live next door to my cousin in Kington St Michael. He had bright green eyes, and I danced with him to Leo Sayers 'When I need you' at a disco and fell in love with him, was absolutely besotted with him. Now I realise I wasn't in love with him, I was in love with the thought of being in love and being saved and rescued. For the next year or possibly more I was crazy about him, and he went out with everyone, but me, he went out with Caroline and Claire, and heavens knows who else but not me.

There were loads of boys around at that time, for everyone else. I always fancied them but I was never good enough to be some ones girlfriend. It was always just a kiss, I could never let them touch me, why would anyone want to touch this? Anyone I kissed could be the one, the one to love me, save me, rescue me from my self-loathing, they could fix me surely?

Then I fell for Niall's friend, Tim, tall, blonde boy who I danced to Rita Coolidges 'We're all alone now' at a Luckington Disco but he wasn't interested in me at all either.

My cousin had a serious bike accident and on the way to visit him with Mum, things were fraught at home again, another affair going on somewhere, she told me that Dad always had affairs when she was pregnant, and that when we were little she'd driven Claire and me to Bristol and knocked on a woman's door, who Dad was having an affair with. With me beside her and Claire in the pushchair she said, "do you know he's married with two kids?"

My friendship with Caroline was sometimes a bit rocky and I saw her walking off up the hill with Jill and Linda one day and was left thinking, "why are you with them? Aren't we friends anymore? What's wrong with me?" It seems we just weren't and I had no idea why we were no longer best friends. But we just weren't. I'd left the Bear and was working at The Rowden Arms as a commis waitress and had met new friends there who were in the top sets. Caroline had a biker boyfriend so maybe our paths had perhaps separated.

I worked at the Rowden while I did my O levels. The owners had a red setter who sat on the stairs all day and was rarely walked so I started to walk him for them and eventually asked them if I could have him and they said yes, so Humphrey Tobevan the Great was our first dog. I walked him every morning around the donkey field on Bristol Road before school. We all liked having a dog, we'd often had cats but Humphrey was much more fun.

I left The Rowden when I was sixteen to work in Woolworths part time. I worked on the sweet counter with Janice and Sharon and we'd walk between the two displays knocking sweets off of the pick'n'mix so they'd break and we could eat them, we were all big and I was getting bigger. There were a few girls from school who worked in Woolworths, most were the year above and some older than that. There was an unwritten rule that when a supervisor left the next girl who had been there longest would be promoted to the job. The manager passed the sweet counter as I was serving an old man one day and the next thing I knew I was the Supervisor which didn't go down too well with the older girls but they did get over it. I liked the job in Woollies, everyone came to Woollies for something, it was a fun place to work.

Punk was beginning to take root, everything's a bit late in Chippenham, and my clothes were becoming a little obscure. Our uniform was blue overalls in Woollies and I recall wearing a green top with a collar that showed and a red and white polka dot skirt that I'd made and was longer than the uniform so showed beneath it, bright yellow tights and purple flat T bar shoes, that I'd dyed from brown, and my hair was always a different shade of auburn/red and I loved make up and using wild eye shadow colours. I had to wear heavy make-up to cover my acne.

My new friends were a bit posh, they were all going to University which I'd never thought about. There were a lot of parties, some in fancy dress, again lots of photos. I recall going to one in a blue plastic see through mac, with a zip up the front, fishnet tights, high black heels and underwear, masses of bright eye shadow, green hair. It rained that night and the dye ran down my face.

I decided to stay on for A levels at school but only lasted three days as I couldn't even understand the language Mr Stuart used in my first Economics lesson so I changed to Chippenham Technical College to do more O Levels as I only got four and four CSEs, hence my lack of knowledge of grammar probably, I am sorry.

COLLEGE

On my first day at Chippenham Tech this tall, curly haired boy walked in wearing a leather jacket and red kickers, Harvey, and he looked a little like Gary Numan, who was Top of the Pops at the time and I drooled. He became friends with all of us. There were lots of parties as there were lots of new people to meet.

At Christmas we all piled into the Railway Pub, Claire came with me and she met Harvey and that was it, they became boyfriend and girlfriend. Mum and Dad didn't like him probably because Claire went on the pill for him at fifteen years old. After college he became unemployed and they hated that, what a layabout he must be, but his mother had moved away and he had a flat in Corsham so Claire would stay there a lot. When she was home constant arguments would ensue with Mum and so Dad would disappear to the Neeld to get out of the way. One day Dad brought Colette, the barmaid, to our house and sat next to her on the sofa. She put her legs over Dad's legs, I was confused, what on earth was going on? He was having another affair.

So then the arguing and screaming and shouting began in earnest between Mum and Dad, and Claire and Mum. I hated him, he kept hurting Mum and yet she kept taking him back and forgiving him, I just couldn't understand it. He was still working away most of the week and when he called if I picked up the phone I'd scream at him, "why don't you fuck off", and the C word would come out, the language in our home had become really, really bad and frequent. Mum did kick him out again but it didn't last long.

At college I'd met and was absolutely smitten with a 6'2" mod called Kevin who I then lost my virginity to one hot summer's night, but I was never his girlfriend, just a girl he used occasionally. He had a girlfriend, a big girlfriend which is probably why I went after him, after all if he'd dated one big girl he might date another. I introduced him to my friend Eddi, from swimming club, and they started going out together and yet I kept seeing him from time to time, unbeknown to her. I was completely besotted, again, with him, and yet I was never the girlfriend.

We went to a party in Dauntsey and when we walked in they stopped the music and put on Yazoo '*Nobody's Diary*' because they thought I was, or looked like Alison Moyet. If only, I loved her.

I passed my driving test in 1980 and Dad insisted I bought a Vauxhall Viva from a local garage for £700 and I became a taxi to everyone.

I fancied Jake who lived around the corner and had a Vauxhall Viva too and we'd all go out in a gang to Lacock drinking and then drive up to Bowden Hill to listen to people on CB radios. I did get to snog Jake a couple of times but that was as far as it got, rarely did I go any further, why would he ever want to touch me? There was always a folk festival too, we'd walk to Lacock, drink until drunk and stagger back to Chippenham, great fun.

I left Chippenham Tech at Christmas in '79 because I realised I wasn't really doing much work, it was all parties. So I got a job at Granada on the M4 at Leigh Delamere in the cash office in January 1980. I worked there for eighteen months, fancying a very beautiful, tall handsome black guy who wasn't the least bit interested in me but I spent £80 on a bottle of Eau Sauvage on him for his birthday, trying to impress and buy him. I realised I wasn't going to go any further in that office so I left and took a job as a trainee accountant at Earle of Chippenham for a year, a Ford Dealership. Around that time I lost a lot of weight, not sure why, perhaps through sheer determination and I became almost anorexic, periods stopped, men took an interest and I got scared.

A local family had opened the old cinema in Chippenham as Goldigger's, a nightclub. I got so drunk there that Christmas Eve I woke up in the broom cupboard at 4am and walked out to find all the cleaners at work. I still drove home though. Nan and Gramp came for lunch and I didn't even leave my bed, Nan knew what I'd done though and was not pleased, "you don't want to be like your Great Grandfather," she said. I was given a packet of eight mars bars in my stocking and ate the lot in ten minutes, thanks Mum.

I later discovered that my Great Grandfather, Nan's father, used to go to Chippenham market on a Friday and sell the ponies he had, he was a trader, and gamble at poker with his earnings and drink. He'd drink so much they'd load him in the cart at the end of the day, slap his horse on the hind and shout, "take 'im 'ome," and the horse would walk all the way back to Tiddleywink with Great Grandad fast asleep in the cart the whole time. He got so drunk one time he gambled the cottage and lost it.

Around this time I went out with Philip, the beautiful blonde boy who had lived opposite us on Cherry Tree Crescent, he was, is, SO beautiful. His ex had arranged the date, I'd worked with her in Woollies and she was trying to help him move on from her, he wasn't the least bit interested in me. I remember sitting on his lap when we he came in for coffee. We didn't go out twice, we didn't even kiss that I recall.

When I turned eighteen I got a job as a barmaid at the Castle in Castle Combe. I'd always wanted to be a barmaid, always thought I was a bit Bet Lynch. From there I went and worked at The Lansdowne Strand in Calne three or four evenings a week while I worked at Earle's. I'd rush home at five grab something to eat and then rush to Calne to work, hygiene wasn't anything I really thought much about, I showered every morning and that was good enough, or so I thought.

When I was at the girl's school I'd wear a pair of pants, then tights, then pants to keep my tights up and our Health Education teacher, would tell us that if we ever had anything wrong, 'down there,' we were dirty. It got very hot down there and would itch so I'd scratch it, by the time I was eighteen it was so painful I went to the doctor who duly said, "slut" when I was still a virgin, had never been touched there by a man. I had vaginal warts. I had to go to Bath RUH Sexual Health Clinic and was really embarrassed. They were only external but the humiliation of putting legs in stirrups was overwhelming and I cried, they went very, very quickly, thank goodness.

I had warts on my fingers and toes too from about sixteen years old, they got really bad, so bad I could barely get my shoes on. At a Darts Presentation Dinner in the Neeld Hall one evening with Caroline, her parents and my Mum and Dad, there was an older lady, Joan there. Dad said, "ask Joan, she'll get rid of them," and three days later they all went, all twenty-five plus of them, I still have mildly inflamed skin where they were though. Magic, just magic, lovely lady.

I did like working in the Lansdowne Strand, there were a group of guys who were regulars and we went to see the Rolling Stones at Wembley in 82, me being the taxi of course, them stoned, but it was a good day out, and we had a few others too. No one I fancied in that gang much though, until one night this bloke came in, curly hair, bit rough around the edges, and I went home with him for coffee, then to his bedroom. Joan Jet and the Blackhearts '*I love rock and roll*' reminds me of him to this day. I stayed in my t-shirt and pants all night, all we did was kiss and cuddle and still he didn't come to the pub again, what was wrong with me? Why do they never come back? They always came back for other girls but never for me.

While I was at Earle's a boy over the road had a friend who looked like the drummer in Kajagoogoo and I fancied him even though he was younger than me. I'd have sex with him on our living room floor, desperate for him to like me and want me. He wasn't interested in me at all, but sex was on offer so he turned up occasionally. I was beginning to realise sex could get me a cuddle and kiss, the price was immaterial, it was the closest I could get to love and yet it was really a million miles from it.

For my twentieth birthday I went with a friend on an 18–30s holiday to San Antonio in Ibiza. We met lots of people and one boy looked liked Harvey, so I fancied him. On my birthday night I drank a whole bottle of Bacardi and was so drunk I had sex with this boy, not that I really remember it. Some months later a girl we'd met on the holiday asked for a picture of me, she said it was for him but it turned out it was for his mates to take the mickey out of him for shagging the fat bird.

I left Earle's and decided to become a trainee manager in a pub so I got a job at a pub in Dorset. I didn't like it after only a few weeks and so came back home and enrolled on a TOPS course to learn shorthand, typing and audio at Trowbridge College. I also got a job as a barmaid in Goldigger's. I liked working there but felt the size of a house compared to the other beautiful dolly birds that were working.

I finished this TOPS course in May and saw an advert in a paper for a Wages Clerk so I called and it was a holiday park in Brean. I got the job, but as a Cash Clerk, and moved there. My last night in Chippenham before moving to Brean we went to Goldigger's and I got very drunk, so drunk I called this friend of Kajagoogoos who I'd always fancied. He was tall, dark and handsome and always had very pretty girlfriends. I asked him for a lift home, so he turned up at Goldigger's on his motorbike with a spare helmet and I duly got on the back in my mid length cotton turquoise and white striped Laura Ashley skirt. He took me to his and it was the most disappointing one night stand, he had a tiny penis, I don't like a small penis at all so was never interested in him thereafter, not that he was in me either. I like a penis to fit, so when I sit on it it has to touch my belly button, or at least feel like it does.

The next day Mum drove me to Brean and we took the old road as it looked more direct than the M4 and M5, it took hours and hours, with a raging hangover, it was a horrible journey.

BILL

The holiday camp was fun, new people, holiday atmosphere. All we did was work, drink, eat and the others had loads of sex, but who would want me? Almost all the girls that worked there put on two or three stone over the summer as we got free takeaways every night after drinking all evening with the other staff and I was no exception.

While I was handing out pay packets one day one of the boys mentioned that, "Bill likes big girls, be careful," and that was it, he was on my radar. He was a bit younger than me but gorgeous square jaw, cheeky, and flattering, a bit stocky but OK. On my birthday we got together and when my work colleague, Linda, left to go to Uni he moved into my shed (we called them that, they were chalets). He was supposed to become a professional footballer which he had been at sixteen, the youngest ever he said, for Bedford Town but they were also the first club to go bust. His great uncle(?) had played for Arsenal and England.

He took a year off because of me and his mates always moaned at him for it, for missing his big chance. We spent the winter going backwards and forwards from Bedford to Chippenham, he didn't drive so I did it all in my red Austin Healy Sprite called Kermit because the registration was KMT... I worked at Goldigger's again in the evenings in the box office as a cashier and The King Alfred at lunchtimes as a barmaid.

There were a gang of boys who would come to Goldigger's regularly because they lived in Chippenham and one of them just caught my attention, although I had noticed him walking home from school holding hands with his girlfriend years earlier. When I saw he had green eyes that did it, as usual. I must've mentioned this bloke a bit too often because Bill was always very jealous of him and yet I never had a chance with him, he was beautiful and I was not in that league. There was another man in the same gang too, who was very quiet but handsome and smiley.

Bill was a very jealous man. He would moan if I wore make up sometimes, or dressed up, "why do you want to look nice, who are you after?" very insecure, or just copying his father perhaps? His mother was lovely, but unwell, on lots of medication, diagnosed schizophrenic and his father drank a bottle of red wine every evening which I thought very odd. His father had written the computer programme for BT directory enquiries. And his uncle and aunt had founded CND in the 60s, we visited them in Forest Gate once. Bill's elder sister had been conceived out of wedlock and the whole family were adamant anti abortionists.

Claire and Harvey had married in 1982, he eventually got a job as a trainee manager in Bejams, and they bought a one-bedroom house in Chippenham for £18000. Mum and Dad were happy with him now that he had a job and Claire had a job in a bank so all was good. I was large, I wore a black dress for the wedding from Wallis, it's in the photos, rare that I'm in front of the camera, very rare, I still hate photographs of me but I am getting a bit better, slowly.

Bill applied to do Maths, Stats and Computing at Thames Poly and got in for the next year. After that first winter at Goldigger's and The King Alfred we got jobs at the same holiday park but at Camber Sands, him as a barman and me as an entertainments cashier working out the bingo and cine racing. I bought him a Bulworker and he got SO fit and was always beautiful, so he got lots of tips, so many tips they thought he was fiddling and sacked him so I left too which they were surprised about because they knew he'd been snogging another girl, but I didn't. We'd earned £50.56pw each and he'd let me have the 56p, and we still managed to get drunk on his night off, so we had savings, he used to say, "you don't know how important it is that we save".

On July 13th 1985 Kerry, Annie and I went to Live Aid, I'm always the one arranging and organising stuff so we were there! It was a long day but oh so good, unforgettable! Humphrey, our red setter, had developed a tumour on his snout and could barely eat. While we were there Mum had him put down. When we got home and I realised I burst into tears screaming, "why didn't you have Nan put down, she's less use," I was SO upset, it really broke my heart.

We moved back to Chippenham and got jobs at Leigh Delamere and then we moved to Catford for him to start his degree. The landlord had dogs that would shit on the stairs so we didn't stay there long and moved to Belmont Hill, Lewisham and I got a job with Beefeater Gin in Kennington doing the payroll. I doubled my salary to £6k per annum with this job and so treated myself to a lovely long cream mac from a designer range, very striking. My boss at Beefeater knew people at Camber and heard that Bill had been sacked and was just awful, so I walked out one day but they moved me to the transport department rather than let me go. Bill and I were rocky, I was going home most weekends and we didn't spend Christmas together which is never a good sign in my view, I didn't like being at his home very much although his Mum was very sweet and kind. So we split and left Belmont Hill and I came home and then after some temping I went back to the holiday park at Brean for another summer season.

This time I met Marie, the camp nurse, from Manchester who was into dieting and drinking and men so we got along well. There was another nurse, Sula, also from Manchester. And there was Lucy, who worked in the cash office with me and lived locally and she'd bring her brother David along for evenings and when he met Sula they became a couple, are married now I think. Lucy and David had moved from Essex when their Dad had taken redundancy from Fleet Street. Lucy was stunning, tiny, long blonde hair, beautiful and she fell for Sula's brother Jordan when he visited. She came to work one day and said, "I want to do this on a ship," so she applied to Royal Caribbean Cruise Liners and a few weeks later went off to the Caribbean to be a Purserette.

Marie hooked up with a good-looking kitchen porter called Biff but it didn't last long because all the other girls were constantly after him, it broke her heart though, the other girls were very jealous of Marie. We became very good friends for years afterwards fuelled by our constant diets, drinking binges and pulling of men, though in reality it only happened once or twice, in Manchester, while I lived with her for six weeks sometime later.

While at the holiday park I visited Cardiff with a friend and we went to the Hilton by the station and I was awestruck, it was all white marble, green planting and waterfalls, I just loved it, so when the season finished I wrote to them and asked if they had any jobs but didn't hear back initially.

I did meet a couple of blokes I fancied at Brean that year who worked there too. I slept with two of them when I was drunk which was pretty much most nights but only ever kissed, would never let them touch, why ever would they want to touch? I liked a welsh guy called Barry, not my sort at all really but desperate times lead to desperate measures, there was no one else I was interested in or thought I was good enough for, he had a girlfriend so I was only ever the other girl that fancied him.

The season ended and I went home and back to Goldigger's and got a temp job in payroll at Avon Rubber in Melksham and then I got a call from the Hilton in Cardiff. So I became a night auditor and moved to Cardiff, on Newport Road, a tiny room with shared bathroom and kitchen but it was OK and I liked the job. One night a few weeks later I'd arranged to go out with the girls from work and there was a knock at my door, it was Bill, so I never went out with the girls and a week or two later I moved back to London with him in Plumstead where he shared a house with four friends from poly. It was there that I fell pregnant, the withdrawal contraception method is not contraception, it doesn't work, those sperm are coming out way before ejaculation. Although to be fair I'd never been on the pill previously either, how I didn't fall pregnant before I don't really know.

Nan died on 23rd May 1987, Gramp had already gone, I didn't really feel that sad, she was old, very old, eighty-three or so and the last time I'd seen her was in Chippenham Cottage Hospital and she was a little odd lady who said peculiar things. The day of her funeral we were all at home in the kitchen and I mentioned that I was pregnant, to which Mum retorted, "I haven't got time for that now," and everything carried on, how could it not. I cried at Nan's funeral but I'm not sure it was for the loss of her.

I now had a job in New Covent Market, doubling my salary again to £12k, delighted, doing book keeping and office work for George who sold fruit and veg there and had a veg prep company in the arches under the railway where the office was. I loved it, and quite liked the electrician Steve, who would spend hours chatting with me.

Bill was insistent that I must keep the baby. I wasn't quite so sure so I came home for the weekend and Mum, Dad, Claire, Kerry, Andy (Kerry's boyfriend) and I went for dinner to the Salutation and it was concluded that it probably wasn't a good idea to have a baby at twenty-five, mainly by Mum who didn't want an unmarried daughter with a child. So I went back to London, sat on the bed next to Bill and said, "if I have this baby and you **ever** leave me I will screw you for every penny you ever earn," to which he replied, "get rid of it". He was determined he was going to earn a fortune, like his father, not that you'd know it.

We left Plumstead and moved to Queens Road in Peckham to a flat which we shared with Marie, the nurse. On the Wednesday of Wimbledon week, which was a boiling hot day, I went to St Georges on Denmark Hill and had a termination, after all it was only like having a tooth out wasn't it, it was no big deal, it was no bigger than a pea.

THE PAIN

A few weeks later I bought the *Vogue Beauty Guide* and was thumbing through it when I came across a chapter on pregnancy. There were pictures of foetuses and my heart sank, at twelve weeks it wasn't a pea at all, he or she was fully formed. I cried, I sobbed, it completely broke my heart and continued to do so for many, many years.

I was going home every weekend. I would leave New Covent Garden at lunchtime and drive down the M4 in my yellow W reg Mini like a bat out of hell, becoming SO angry if anything was in front of me holding me up, it was a very stressful drive, very, very busy. When I got home I'd go to open the back door and it would be locked. I'd go mental when Mum let me in and remember being curled up in a ball on the floor in floods of tears screaming, "I wish I were a prostitute, perhaps then I'd feel loved," I felt like I was going crazy. My food was going the other way, I was losing weight.

I bumped into Caroline who invited me to her forthcoming wedding which I went to the reception of, she was marrying another biker and the reception was at the Bear Hotel where we'd worked. They had a bungalow in Melksham and regularly had parties where I met her friend Philip, who I wanted more than Bill, and that was when we finished and he moved out. Marie and I got another lodger, or was it two?

I was very slim now and working from midnight until 4pm daily to catch up on all the accounts that hadn't been done in years for George. I'd get the coffees for the men on the stall and as I walked through the market I'd be wolf whistled at and the men would call out, "alright Linda," because I looked a bit like Linda Lusardi who was a page 3 model. I liked working those hours, stopped me being bored. George let me have my own fruit and veg stall and gave me £350pw cash so I was earning the equivalent of £50kpa in 1987. I was the only female salesperson in New Covent Garden market. I did hear later there was another but I never met her. It was great working with two thousand men, I enjoyed it, but I was still single. I fancied a couple of men at the market but they didn't seem interested in me at all.

Marie and I would go up west on a Tuesday night to a club just off of Oxford Street sometimes and one time we met Claire's boyfriend, Alan and his mates. By this time she was divorced and now dating this Met copper from Chippenham. Years earlier I'd been out with Alan once, to the Dumb Post, but not again, he was rather overweight then but not now, but he still wasn't interested in me even then. When he mentioned to his mate that he was dating Claire his mate had said, "the fat one?", no, Claire wasn't the fat one. This night I copped off with his very lovely mate, with the gorgeous kiss, Rick, and went back to their digs but didn't stay long once his hand wandered where it wasn't wanted. But Alan had been kissing another girl all night?

Caroline and her hubby had a New Year's Eve party and I met Mark, from Chippenham, he lived in London, only a few miles from me so we started going out, which was really nice. He picked me up once and had bought me flowers, so kind, but I couldn't bear the fact that he actually liked me and so had to end it after only a few weeks.

I was still going home every weekend and going out and getting very drunk and usually ending up at Goldigger's with Claire and other friends and Pete, the man with the very green eyes was usually there. I noticed him looking at me now that I was slim so in the bit on the side (a smaller bar at the club) I walked up to him as he was ordering drinks and said, "mine's a wine and soda", he was rather taken aback but bought my drink. From then on that evening he looked at me more so later we danced to a slow one and kissed. Oh my god, that kiss, it's always about the kiss. It was February 1988, now that date I do remember because I was slowly going crazy and this poor man just landed in the middle of it. He walked me home that night, which took ages because I just wanted to snog him the whole time. When we got home I made coffee, we went into the living room, I sat on his lap and during the conversation I said, "don't like me because I don't like me".

I was determined that this man was going to wait for sex, I was not going to let this end like the few others I'd met who weren't interested at all and I was convinced it was because I'd had sex too early on, but there had only been six for heaven's sake. So I kept coming home every weekend and seeing Pete at the end of the evening, playing games of chase all night around the pubs, trying to catch him looking at me. I gave him my number but he never called. I tried to make him miss me by not coming home for weeks at a time and then turning up out of the blue. This went on for years, literally years, I was absolutely besotted with him, completely and utterly love addicted to him, poor thing. I did make him wait the six months for sex though, blow jobs don't count do they?

After a year or so I decided to move back home, to see if I could make it work as a relationship, not that he wanted it in the slightest, he'd already sussed I was crazy and was trying to avoid me at all costs but I don't give up easily.

I left George and got a job as PA to a Director of an insurance company in Bristol, I had the interview in London and the woman who met me instantly said, "he'll like you," and I got the job. I had this lovely dark navy long Laura Ashley coat with a single button, it did look very elegant, not a word that usually describes me. I met Nick, he'd grown up on the same street as an older pop singer and said of him, "he only ever gave piano lessons to boys," and of a certain politician that it was known he was the head of the biggest paedophile ring in the UK, we were going to get along just fine.

He travelled a lot as they were planning to open in Australia so I'd take him to Heathrow and then he'd let me use his brand new E reg 750il BMW while he was away, lovely car. He asked me to meet him at the Lancaster Hotel on his return from Australia a few weeks after I started working for him, to catch up on all the post etc and said I might as well stay and we could get dinner too, sounded very lovely to me. Two bottles of Perrier Jouet later I swear the Lancaster was a ship as I tried to walk to my room, with him escorting me and when he made a move to kiss me I shrieked, "oh my god I've always wanted a sugar Daddy but I'm in love with someone else and just can't", our professional relationship and his liking of me went downhill thereafter.

When he was away he gave me tickets he had for stuff, I took a friend to see Bon Jovi in corporate hospitality at the NEC which was OK but I wasn't really a fan. He also gave me four tickets for the Conservative Party Ball at the Grosvenor House Hotel on Park Lane but I couldn't go, I was far too fat to go to that so I gave the tickets to Claire and Alan who duly got very drunk but had a great time with friends.

I moved to Hotwells in Bristol and lodged with Mary, we became friends and one sunny Friday after work we went to the Avon Gorge hotel that overlooks Clifton Suspension bridge. There were a group of very good-looking men there, all suited and booted, who we got chatting to. The next night we'd arranged to go to Goldigger's, as she'd never been, and they all turned up unexpectedly. Pete looked on, a little surprised but I liked rubbing his nose in it and we weren't speaking anyway, we only spoke when we were together which was very rare. Three of these men wanted a lift home in the BMW, so we obliged and on the M4 at 2am I looked at the speedometer and we were doing 180mph, it felt like 70mph, nice car.

The weight came back on so I would stay away from Chippenham for weeks at a time, with the crazy belief that I'd lose X amount of weight, turn up and woo Pete back, which I did sometimes, but it was only ever for a night. Once Jo, Mum's cousin, was over from San Francisco and all the family went out for dinner and then Claire and I went to Goldigger's, I was wearing a very striking white shirt with large black polka dots and black trousers. Dad and I had a nice picture taken at this dinner that night, in a very lovely upstairs restaurant in Corsham. It's still in a frame, one of the only pictures of me in my home. When we got to Goldigger's Pete and I got together and we smooched while his mate held Heather, a friend of mine back, he'd been dating her but I didn't know that at the time. I brought him back to Bristol that night for amorous unrivalled passion. I understand his mates cheered when he turned up in the pub wearing the same suit the next day. The next week I turned up again and he was with Heather, the girl he'd been dating and wasn't interested in me in the slightest. I got very, very drunk and walked over while he was with her and asked him to come home with me, to which he said, "no".

I went home, drove as usual, and took an over dose, I'd had enough, I didn't want to live a moment longer, I was never good enough, there's always something wrong with me, life will never be good, I will never be loved, stop the planet, I want to get off.

The words of Yvonne Elliman '*If I can't have you*' I don't want nobody baby, always remind me of him and this time. The next morning I awoke to the sound of a siren, we lived on the same road as the fire station. I didn't know you couldn't overdose with Nurofen.

Another time he pissed me off so much I poured a whole pint of beer over his head in Goldigger's, he was not happy. I could recount every night I spent with him, as there were really so very few over five years, but I was completely and utterly besotted with him. Everybody that knew me knew I was in love with Pete and he was 'the one' as I'd seen Madam Tamar, a psychic, and she'd told me I was going to meet him in six weeks or six months. I replied, "can't it be six days?" and she said she didn't think so, but I kissed him six days later and that was it. I was just SO desperate to be loved and he was SO loving when we were together, I felt so safe when he wrapped his arms and legs around me all night, I was going to be his girlfriend one day, and wife the next, and of course, I was never either.

I did realise something was wrong, so much so that my doctor got me an appointment for a psychiatric assessment at the Maudsley, opposite St Georges where I'd had the termination. My eating was completely off the wall, I put the weight I'd lost back on rapidly and all I wanted to do was get drunk and get pregnant, not that I realised that consciously. I ballooned to almost seventeen stone. There was a photo but I destroyed it. These were not happy times and I couldn't figure out why I couldn't stop eating and getting very drunk and wanted to sleep with so many men, though sleep was something I didn't do if I was with a man.

I saw another, or a few psychics around this time, desperate for hope, hope that I'd be loved someday. One told me I'd meet an older wealthy man who would change the rest of my life, to which I asked if I'd marry him? "No, he'll already be married". "You're going on a journey, a journey around yourself," a gypsy on the High Street in Bath told me after taking a fiver. "You're going to travel, a lot...you're going to fall pregnant three times but have two children... you're going to work from home with your husband doing something with a calculator...you're never going to want for anything...you'll have two husbands... you're not dying in this country and you're going to live where you can hear the waves on a beach," others have told me, I'm still waiting for the second husband and the last bit, I wish. When life isn't happy they give me hope that's all, they usually only tell me good stuff and when I'm down hope is all I need.

I did get in to bed with a few men and get straight out, saying, "no, I'm in love with someone else". I did see a friend of Pete's and my sisters, Jerry, who I liked, he was clever, intelligent, I like that, Pete wasn't that, he didn't even know who Neil Kinnock was. Pete was a plasterer, loads of money, beautifully turned out and good looking, SO good looking to me. I occasionally went home with Jerry, he was just nice, bit small where it mattered to me, nice kiss though, and tactile. Jerry's best friend was Ed, Ed was full of himself, and had a very small penis a friend told me after she slept with him, but he was very cruel and used to call me rhino. We went ten pin bowling one time and he put my name up as rhino, not a nice man. Some years later I heard he'd had a penis enlargement; I wonder if they work? Around this time too I did once proposition a friend of Claire's when she stayed over, frightened her apparently, I was very drunk, I do apologise and did so then I'm sure.

I left Nick and the insurance company to go into sales but didn't like it and when I was out driving to see customers I'd binge chocolate, biscuits and cake as usual, constantly, so the weight was piling on. Nick married his next PA.

I decided to return to London to live in a five bedroom flat with Claire, Rachel, Andy and Mike on Blackstock Road at the end of Gillespie Road where Arsenals stadium was, so every other Saturday there were thousands of supporters about. We went a couple of times, spent £3 getting in and stood in the stand behind the goal propped up on a railing with a pint in our hand, bored stiff. It was 1989 though so was an exciting time for Arsenal I think, not that we realised it.

Dad and me 1989

THE BOOK

I'd applied for lots of jobs to move back to London and the agency for this one job was surprised that the employer asked for a handwritten letter of application and then only wanted to see me. I wasn't anywhere near as qualified as the other candidates but I got the job. It was as a PA/Office Manager for a property company in Kensington Gardens. Months after I started the job in November 1989 I realised why, he had a private drawer in his desk that no-one was allowed to go near but when he lost some cash and was ranting for a week about it I opened the drawer and there was the cash. But there was also a report, he'd had my handwriting analysed by an old lady and it was absolutely fascinating, wish I'd copied it really but I didn't. The thing I remember most was it said I was 'loyal to the job, not necessarily the employer' which I thought was odd but interesting. She also said she couldn't understand why my writing was so big, I now wonder if it was anger? It also said I was very thorough, honest, reliable, organised, trustworthy, kind, caring and would get a job done. I like to think that was really why I got the job.

Saul told me he was 'a Saudi Arabian Jew', Jerry later told me you can't be one of those, I had no clue. He was a very wealthy man, his daughter had just married into an even wealthier Jewish family. He had a son, Ben, a few years younger than me, absolutely beautiful man, dating a blonde Patsy Kensit type, with a child, of which his father really didn't approve. Camilla worked for him, as did a Lord and an MP who had had an affair with an actress, a very attractive actress, and it had been all over the front page of The Sun. One day the MP turned up to the office in a brand spanking new Mercedes SL very pleased with himself, there was a waiting list for them apparently. A few minutes later, Henry, Ben's brother in law, twenty plus years the MPs junior turned up in the largest top of the range of the same car, the MP was embarrassed, but it was rather funny.

A week or two after I started working for Saul he asked why was I so big to which I replied, "oh it comes and goes," and he was concerned about my acne so sent me to his private doctor who gave me tablets and it just went, in days. Later he held out a book which he gave to me and said, "read the first 126 pages of this and take out the words alcohol and alcoholism and put in food and compulsive overeater". I was a bit taken aback but glad as I knew I had a problem with food, I was almost seventeen stone after all. The book was the Big Book of Alcoholics

Anonymous. I read the first 126 pages that weekend and sobbed. Every day I was battling with food, starving until just before lunchtime and then bingeing anything but mostly foods with sugar and flour in.

On weekends for months and months I wasn't going out with flat mates, I was buying a bag of food and bingeing it. I'd have a large packet of digestives, a packet of milk chocolate digestives and a packet of golden crunch and I'd dunk the lot in hot tea. I'd have to wait a bit for that to go down and then I'd start on a large sliced white loaf covered with butter and marmalade, jam or sugar, or even tomato ketchup, or a large box of muesli with milk and sugar. When that was all digested and far enough down in my stomach I'd finish with two or three large bars of chocolate and a litre and a half of diet coke, because I was always dieting, of course, didn't you know. I'd barely be able to move after consuming it all and so would sleep to get rid of it, feeling SO sick, hoping and praying that I'd explode in the night and never wake up. Please God, if there is one, take me now, stop this misery and emotional pain, please, please stop it, help me please, let me go.

Ben had a beautiful apartment which had been featured in a glossy magazine. He had a party there and we had all sorts of the rich and famous calling to confirm they were going to be coming, Eric Clapton and Simon Le Bon to name a couple and I was invited but I couldn't go, I just couldn't bring myself to go to a party like that when I looked like this. I did go to the Christmas party though because Saul insisted, at Tramp, in Mayfair, took Rachel, Claire's friend along. Had sausage and mash and hid as much as I could. It was OK just watching more of the rich and famous, don't think I danced at all though, far too embarrassed to move from my seat.

In the Big Book there were these steps, steps that would cure me of what I now knew was an eating addiction, just like an alcohol addiction or drug addiction. So I called Caroline and asked her to come up for the weekend so that we could do these steps. We sat on my bed this Saturday afternoon, looked at these steps and I said, "well I don't believe in God so we'll miss out all of that, there's nothing in my past that's a problem so we won't have to do that searching and fearless moral inventory thing and we can miss out that and that and that," and we looked at each other and said, "that's quite a lot, never mind, come on, let's go to the pub", so we did, and got very drunk, again.

Saul wasn't that nice a man, he brushed past me so close one day he pressed up against my breast and I felt very, very uncomfortable. He seemed to know a lot about addiction, but I didn't know why. He packed Camilla, the secretary, off to a rehab in Kent for sex addiction because she'd slept with Henry. I didn't really get it but was curious about this place near Canterbury in Kent and discovered it was the only rehab in the country that addressed food as an addiction. The more I read the stories in the back of the Big Book the more I related to them and realised I had an addiction problem, to sugar and flour at least. There was another fellowship called Overeaters Anonymous but I could find very little about it anywhere, in truth I didn't know where to look and was too embarrassed to ask.

My relationship with Saul was fraught, I felt like he wanted to own me, control me, tie me to him which I really didn't like and so one day in April I'd had enough and left. He already had his next muse, Sara, a very pretty eighteen-year-old who he employed alongside me, just like he had me alongside Camilla. The PA in the chair in front of the window changed quite regularly I learned. Just before I left he'd taken health insurance on me and I knew that was how he'd funded Camilla in rehab and I wanted to go, so I went back and almost on bended knees begged him to allow me to use that insurance to get to this rehab, and reluctantly he did.

Mum and Dad moved from Aylesbury Road to Oakfields, to a lovely three-bedroom cottage in May of 1990 and on May 12th, Pete's birthday, Mum and Aunty Jean drove me from Chippenham to Kent. We stopped in Reading at M&S and I bought a size twenty cream long polyester, satin feel dressing gown, I still have it.

I went to rehab for my food addiction, all I wanted to do was lose weight, but they insisted I had an alcohol problem too so I acknowledged that when I drank I always drank to get drunk and, "off the planet," so maybe? I'd have done anything at that point to stop overeating, and I did, do whatever they told me, including believe in God which I'd never done. The rows Caroline and I would have about Catholicism, and why would anyone ever think a blonde haired, blue eyed MAN was in charge of the universe, WHY? Religion to me had been created to keep women, the poor and uneducated in check and it was working tremendously well for those men in charge. But I needed something, I needed to stop the suicidal thoughts of, "get me off this planet, please let me explode and be no more," I needed to believe I was worthy of life, I was meant to be here, and loved, so I jumped on the 'God loves me' bandwagon as instructed.

I spent three and a half months in rehab, working up to step five and all paid for by one health insurance premium of £12. I loved it, I loved that my food was controlled, 301, three meals a day, nothing in between, one day at a time and no sugar or flour, I loved the people because they all got me, they all understood.

There were some really hard bits, really hard. One day there was going to be a grieving session, but I had no one to grieve, Nan had been a good age when she'd died and I'd not lost anyone else. In this session we all sat around in a circle, as usual, and were given a glass of water and told to drink half of it, no idea why. And then something was said and I just completely fell apart, crumbled and sobbed, I sobbed so much I could barely breathe, my face started to go red and my eyes puffy. I was taken to the two chairs facing each other in the middle of the circle and told to speak to who I'd lost and of course, it was my child. I'd called her Rosie as my Great Grandparents are in Castle Combe graveyard and they're Rosie and Frederick and if I had children I wanted them to be Rosie and Fred and a psychic had told me it was a daughter I'd terminated. I spoke to her in that moment, told I loved her SO much and was SO sorry, but of course I had to have her tell me it was alright in my mind, it never has been, I can still feel that pain and regret and guilt if I choose to, but I can choose and I chose this life, not that one, however heartbreaking that is, it's a decision I made that I have to live with.

That was one of those monumental light bulb moments in my life, when I accepted what I'd done and started to forgive myself, I don't honestly know if I'll ever forgive myself completely as when I think of it I can still feel immense pain but I deal with it a little better now.

I realised in rehab that I was also a love addict, and I had a problem with men in authority and that I was still addicted to Pete currently, believing if I had him in my life it would be perfect. In the same way that if I were slim everything would be perfect, so I wrote a no send letter to my love addiction and was cured, not. But I've realised that when I put food down I use my love addiction. I think we all need and use something to fix us, we're all addicts, it's just alcohol and non-prescribed drugs are seen as bad addictions, and they do often affect people around you in a detrimental way so no doubt that's why we all dislike those addictions so intensely.

While I was in rehab we had a family counselling session, Mum and Dad came all the way from Chippenham for this session. We sat down with my counsellor and he asked how they thought I was doing and they were pleased, I'd lost weight, was happy. I was glowing, my hair was SO shiny and I was well. Then the counsellor said to Mum, "so why, at three months old, did you stop cuddling Nicola?" to which she replied, "she didn't want to be cuddled, she didn't like it", so I looked at her and said, "so at three months old I looked up at you and said 'don't cuddle me, I don't like it?'", with that Dad's arms flew up above his head and he said, "come on, we're going", and that was it, end of family therapy session.

Mum had always told me I didn't like being cuddled and hugged, so I had asked her why she didn't cuddle me, I knew the answer she'd give. Dad had a habit of throwing his toys out of the pram, arms going up above his head, part of the Swan temper my mother and sister used to ridicule me about that I'd inherited.

I left rehab in late August and was advised by them, "don't go back to where you came from". So I moved to Maida Vale to a halfway house but I only stayed three days, I wanted to go home, to get all that love I'd never had, to see Pete now I was slim and turn his head and it was Mum and Dad's thirtieth wedding anniversary at the end of August and I was organising a secret party for them with Claire and Kerry.

They loved the party, Dad cried and Mum was over the moon, a hundred or more people on their lawn waiting for them as I sped around the corner with Mum saying, "what are all these cars here for", then pulling up to a sharp stop next to the garden where a loud cheer went up, it was a lovely evening.

I took a bit of rehab's advice and didn't take a stressful job. Life was going to be just perfect, I would get Pete as a proper boyfriend now that I was better, slim, happy, normal, I hadn't quite sussed the love addiction stuff.

BACK TO LIFE

But of course that's just not it, losing the weight, stopping drinking or any other addiction just leaves emotional pain without medication or sedation and coping doesn't last long alone, which is why people tend to stick with the fellowship for years and years, it keeps us well.

I was going to OA meetings in Bristol a couple of nights a week but it was hard and I wasn't buying that I really had an alcohol problem so I didn't think I could go to AA. There's no joy in food addiction, there's no laughter, there's no outrageous antics, just pure misery when your stomach is so full you can barely move and all you want to do is be sick or sleep off a binge. I'd learnt how to be sick in rehab from the anorexics. Rehab is like a prison without doors, you can leave whenever you want but you don't want to because you want to be well. Prisons only make better criminals.

Suffice to say the week before Christmas I went to a ball in Swansea with a man I'd met in Goldigger's, Lawri, we were just friends but I liked him, he had a limp but wasn't bad looking, 6'+, was in Financial Services and I was always interested in that field so when he asked I said yes. We dropped our stuff off at his friend's hotel on the Gower, it was pitch black, quickly got changed and raced off to this ball because we were late. I wore a Frank Usher white with black polka dots gown that I'd bought before rehab so I had to take it in four inches each side and it looked stunning, even if I do say so myself, gave me an hour glass figure, had a flamenco style hem, up at the front, down at the back, and when I walked down stairs his eyes lit up. We were having dinner at this ball and he said, "have a glass of prosecco, it's only one", and that was it, I don't remember the rest of the evening at all. Woke up the next morning with fabulous views of the bay and the worst hangover ever, had been sick apparently, not that I could remember it at all, couldn't remember a damn thing. But that was the beginning of the slippery slope back to food addiction, and I was perhaps aware that I might have a bit of an alcohol problem but I didn't want to admit it.

I got a couple of temp jobs and one was at an aggregates firm in Frome and when I'd cleared the aged debt they asked me to stay permanently. I did stay although they knew I was planning to go travelling in June with Claire because Alan had finished with her to go out with the girl he was snogging at the nightclub on Oxford Street that night.

I went out one night with the girls in the department, it was someone's hen night or birthday I think, we went to Longleat, there was a nightclub there, I'd never been before. I wore a mini skirt suit, with a white shirt and heels, I've got good legs. I was nervous, not that I ever realised it, I always drank to hide my nerves especially in new company, surely these people didn't really like me, they couldn't could they? And if they did they clearly didn't know me very well. So I drank too much, as usual, and found a very good looking 6' guy, called Nick I think, who played cricket for some county and was there with all his mates. I snogged his face off and then was desperate to be cuddled so pleaded with him to take me home to his hotel, so his mates bundled me in their car and when I made it clear there wasn't going to be a gang bang, despite being drunk, they drove me to the where I was staying and kicked me out of the car shouting, "whore, slut, slag," as they drove away.

My eating was becoming worse and worse and now I could purge too, but I didn't like doing it, it hurt when my nails scraped the back of my throat, along with the blood shot eyes, it was a horrible experience. I was working back at Goldigger's, saving frantically for my trip. Claire had met Steve and was no longer coming with me, she was moving in with him near Bristol.

AROUND THE WORLD

I bought my around the world ticket for £938 and on June 5th 1991 Mum and Dad drove me, thirteen stone again, to Heathrow with my rucksack to board my first flight to New York. I arrived and after hours I found my hostel, the cab had dropped me at the wrong one so I trudged around New York until I found the right one. I settled down for the night in a dorm with seven girls who were out. When I awoke in the morning I got chatting to the girl on the bunk next to me and her uncle was one of my Mum's employers from some years previously. It's a very small world when you get out in it. I spent five days in New York but didn't contact Mum and Dad, I wanted them to worry, to care, because I never thought they did. When I did get in touch they were relieved. They'd given me a card from BT that I could call them on from anywhere in the world and it would be charged to their phone bill so I really had no excuse for not calling but I wanted to hurt them because I felt that they always hurt me and I knew no better way of doing so.

From New York I flew to Miami where I stayed with Cassie, a friend of Rachel's, who was now living with the man who had given her a job in a market in Miami when she'd gone travelling a couple of years before. She never got any further than Miami and is still there now, divorced with two children I think. From Miami I flew to San Francisco where I stayed with Mum's cousin Jo, lovely, lovely lady. She had an apartment on Bush St. She'd been walking down Oxford St in London in the 60s and saw an advert, £10 to Canada, so she went in and emigrated, she was now in her sixties or seventies, had worked in the oil industry most of her life, had travelled everywhere, including the Galapagos islands. She worked in the big hotel on the side of the lake in Banff, Canada, for a while when she first arrived. I spent a week or so with her, lunching at Fishermans Wharf, going over Golden Gate Bridge, visiting the Great Sequoia National Park to name a few things we did, loved it all.

I liked it there so much I got a job as a Nanny for some realtors in Berkeley with three children. It only lasted a few weeks because they lost a large contract. While I was there Robert Palmer was playing in San Diego, I liked him, I always dreamed of being one of the women in the 'Addicted to Love' video, who didn't? I think The Power Station were his backing band that night but I was never a Duran Duran fan, I was never pretty enough to be a Duranny, I was always on the ugly bench.

From San Francisco I went down to LA, awful place, expected such glam, Hollywood was a dump and Venice Beach wasn't great either, perhaps it's a great place if you're loaded, but as a back packer? So I didn't stay long and got on the next flight to Hawaii.

Hawaii was beautiful, but Waikiki beach was full of body beautifuls and I didn't like being there. I got a bus up to where the world surfing championships were held but it wasn't October so there weren't any thirty-foot waves. I've always wanted to see those. I stayed in a hostel and a guy who was backpacking was flying to Auckland in a day or two so I decided to go with him.

On arrival in New Zealand I decided to do the Kiwi Experience with two girls I'd met on the flight and a load of others so spent a few weeks in New Zealand. Visited loads, we travelled right down to Dunedin and back up to 100-mile beach, hiked around Goat Island, Christchurch was lovely, Milford Sound was so stunning, Queenstown was stunning too. From there we did the awesome foursome, a helicopter ride, bungy jump over Skippers Canyon, white water rafting and took a speed boat down Shotover canyon. We went to Franz Joseph, a glacier and most people walked up it, I couldn't be bothered and so stayed on the bus, got a bag of food and binged. We also did a glow worm thing where you sat in tyres and went along an underground stream with millions of them above your head, spectacular, I think near Rotorua which stank because of the sulphur but was great to see. We saw *'Terminator 2'* in a really old cinema and all the audience were dressed in black, very goth, literally all of them, weird. And the climax was a 10,000-foot freefall parachute jump, with the world champion skydiver on my back, where you could see the east and west coast, amazing, just amazing experience, love a bit of freefalling! They played the song by Tom Petty on the way, always reminds me of it.

Then it was on to Sydney where I visited Mum's cousin who was something to do with films she'd said. It turned out he was the Barry Norman of Australia, had his own TV show. I went to Leura to visit them for a weekend, lovely place but their house had a tin roof, as many did, and when it rained at night it was really noisy. Anthony was married to Sally, younger and lovely, she had an eighteen-year-old son. One night he'd come home and there were lots of people for dinner, when they left he said, "do you know who that was?" and Anthony replied, "yes of course, it was the team from *'Buster'*", "Anthony, that was Phil Collins of Genesis". Anthony had no clue that he was a pop star but Sally's son did.

From Sydney I bussed it to Melbourne, up to Adelaide and on to Ayers Rock where it rained, so I have pictures of Ayers Rock black, which it only goes a few days a year. Again, I didn't want to climb it, rather binge, a daily occurrence by now. From there I went to Catherine

Gorge and up to Darwin where there was a notice on a board, Cook wanted, so I called them and got the job, that was something I knew I could do quite well, I'm a fairly good cook, but my children don't agree. So I got on a bus going west thinking I was going a couple of hundred miles maybe but when I got there and saw a map I was as far west and north as you could get without falling off the edge.

Mardie, was a sheep station. There was an old man Paul who owned the place, Sam his thirty-year-old female assistant ran it, a Jackaroo, and the cook, who wanted to be a Jackaroo, or Jillaroo, so they needed another cook. It was very remote, never saw anyone. A vicar visited once and a helicopter brought in two blokes one time but that was it. Everything we ate was mutton or pumpkin, did lots with mutton and pumpkin, not together. Mum sent me the recipe for chocolate crunch and that was a real hit. Paul employed two aboriginals, there were a few of them nearby, he never knew which two would turn up but he employed two of them daily.

I had to be up to make breakfast for them all before they went off and provide them with packed lunches and a hot meal on their return. I also had to clean the homestead where Paul lived. We all lived in chalets (sheds) nearby. I moved my bed outside on to the veranda because if you slept inside you heard cockroaches on the lino at night and I didn't like that. If I had time to myself while they were out in the day I'd lay on my bed and read a book, though what it was I have no idea. Or I'd write my diary and the butcher birds would come and sit on the wire fence right next to me and sing, and they sang beautifully. At night the sky was so bright with stars it was beautiful and all upside down compared to home and the water went down the plughole the other way too. When I cleaned I'd spray cockroach killer down the plugholes and go back ten minutes later and the bath would have loads wriggling cockies in it and some of them could fly, vile things, just vile. It was so hot when you showered you couldn't get dry, you just dripped of sweat but at least it was clean sweat.

My eating was off the wall and I wasn't happy really. U2's 'Angel of Harlem' reminds me of this time, singing and dancing around the kitchen to it when no one was around. Then I got a birthday card from Bill that Mum forwarded to me. The Jackaroos left and I was alone with Paul and Sam and they thought I was lazy because I'd managed to do in two or three hours what my predecessor had taken all day to do, I can be very efficient. An argument ensued after I started reading the bible that the vicar had given me and I resigned. That night Paul and Sam drove me to the bus stop, it was miles and there were huge kangaroos all the way on the road. I'd already decided to cut my trip short and come home. I was massive, bingeing, alone and miserable.

Mum's cousin's son, a rather spoilt only child who could do no wrong in his parents' eyes, had blown his mother's and the dogs' head off with a twelve bore shot gun, and then his own nearby. Mum could do with some support. I spent a couple of days in Perth, which was lovely and where everything was called Swan, after the river, and then I flew home.

Mum and Claire picked me up at Heathrow and I remember driving along the M4 on this miserable afternoon wondering what life would offer now.

SIMON

Bill and Ben, who I knew vaguely had bought the wine bar in town and had no one to run it during the day so I got the job. It was a job I'd always wanted to do, full time in a bar. This bar was frequented by all the motorway lot who I also knew somewhat vaguely but they were notorious in Chippenham for drinking and other stuff. It didn't take me long to realise that some of them would spend all day, literally ALL day in the bar, from 11–11. Pete would appear at weekends and I'd still be swooning, the weight gain didn't stop me although I felt that I was even less worthy of this beautiful man's attention which I didn't get anyway.

Ben invited me to London to see Starlight Express so I went, on a friend basis. It was OK, I didn't know any of the songs, but the roller skating was watchable. A few days later a colleague mentioned that Ben fancied me, so I had to leave, just couldn't bear it, the thought of someone liking me, but he did have other girlfriends so it was no big deal. How could anyone fancy me, I was enormous?

I went back to temping and spent Christmas back at another holiday park near Weston Super Mare which was pretty dire. After that I took a temp job in Bristol for a pub chain doing credit referencing for prospective landlords.

In June I walked into the Royal Oak on London Road and Mike, Eddi's husband, beckoned me over and introduced me to Simon, Eddi's cousin from Australia so I said, "hi, big country a lot of nothing," and he laughed. The next night I was going out with Eddi and she called to say Simon was over and they were going out with all the family as he was here and I was still welcome to come along, so I did. There was a largish crowd of us in the Pack Horse that evening and I have never laughed so much in my life. It was a great evening. We all went back to Eddi's Mum and Dad's afterwards for coffee and at about eleven, it was a Sunday so the pub had shut at ten, I said I had to go. Simon jumped to his feet and said, "I'll walk you", to which I replied, "don't be daft it's right over the other side of town, I'm fine", "no," he said, "I'll walk you". We got as far as the first hotel, the Angel, and he got a room and stripped off. I stayed fully clothed and told him all about how I was in love with Pete. We talked all night and he asked me to meet him that evening, he was having a farewell drink with Mike but would love to see me before he flew back to Australia on Tuesday morning. I had no other plans so why not. I knew he was in a long-term relationship but not married and we seemed to really get on, so why not indeed. I walked into our bathroom that Monday morning and Mum said, "where have you been?" I looked at her and said, "I think I'm going back to Australia".

I turned up at the Pack Horse at 9.30 and Mike was surprised to see me but smiled and left a while later. I don't know what we did, we didn't sleep together, I know that, we may have kissed, I can't recall, but we just talked and talked and talked. The next day he flew back to Australia. A few days later I got a very lengthy letter that he'd written the whole twenty odd hours of his flight, still have it, in my box somewhere. So I wrote back and then we called each other and he mentioned his partner was going to the Maldives for a couple of weeks with a bloke they'd had threesomes with, so I piped up, "how about I come over while she's away", he was excited by this prospect and so a few weeks later I boarded a plane back to Sydney.

He picked me up at the airport and we drove to Newcastle where he lived. He was a bit paranoid about neighbours seeing me but it was a detached house in a very leafy street so it wasn't that difficult to get in and out. We went out for dinner a lot, and to Port Mcquarie for a weekend which was nice but the two weeks flew by and I left to come home, stopping at Singapore and travelling the length of Indonesia for three of four weeks on a bus. Went to the Gili islands, Borbudur, Keli-mutu, Kamodo Island and everywhere in between, wonderful place, gorgeous people. Skipped over Bali, didn't want to be where all the body beautifuls were, far too fat for that.

Stayed in Singapore a few days and a fortune teller old man sitting outside Raffles Hotel, cross legged on a carpet told me I wouldn't be truly happy until my mid to late fifties, not really what I wanted to hear at almost thirty years old but hey ho.

I arrived back in the UK and instantly thought, why on earth did I come back here, I'm really not staying and so as soon as I could I went back. Pete in the meantime had met, married and had a child with a girl I went to primary school with so that was well and truly done too. Tina Turner's '*Simply the best*' still reminds me of him as well as Barry White's '*You're my first, my last, my everything*'.

Simon was very close to Mike and felt sorry for him because he was sure Eddi was playing away, so much so he told me to sleep with him, I'd always fancied him so I didn't take much persuading. What staggered me was that Mike wanted to sleep with me! I was still very good friends with Eddi though and I'm not a liar so that was difficult, some things are best left not said. One evening Eddi and I went out and I dropped her back at her mum's. I'd arranged to go over and stay with Mike. We were talking in their kitchen when Eddi turned up unexpectedly, she was not happy, we made the excuse that I was missing Simon and so wanted to chat to Mike, she didn't believe it one bit but didn't say so. I left. We've never spoke since.

I was in constant contact with Simon about returning and he was very up for it, delighted in fact, of course he was, he'd have an affair on tap. I flew back going via Bangkok and travelled to Koh Samui for a week or two, which was lovely. Met a German girl and shared a hut on the beach for 25p a night. We left the door open the first night because it was so hot and woke up to find a pack of very scabby dogs sleeping next to us, we never left the door open again. From there I travelled down through Malaysia to Singapore and flew on to Sydney.

I arrived with a suit and heels and went to agencies to find work. Simon's accountant got me a tax number so I was treated like a normal citizen and only had to leave when my visa ran out every three months, so I went to Auckland for lunch with Tony who'd emigrated there from Chippenham after dating the Kiwi barmaid from The Rose and Crown and marrying her.

I got a job with the Australian Wheat Board as an accountant which was a complete farce because I wasn't that qualified, wasn't qualified at all and I struggled to do the work but it paid well so I stayed as long as I could. I moved into a large townhouse with four or five Australians in Randwick right next to a park. It was a lovely place to live, big bedroom, nice-ish people and Simon was in touch daily.

He was older than me, thirteen years older than me and I felt cared for, and loved, so anything he suggested I was up for to please him, however demeaning it was, so a swingers club was first on his list, on the outskirts of Sydney. He got me to dress in lingerie which I'd never done before so felt quite uncomfortable, but it was OK because I was with him. There were twenty or so people there, but I didn't realise most of the women were prostitutes and the other men thought all the women were prostitutes so when one put his hand on my leg and I moved away he wasn't too happy, but Simon explained. It seemed what Simon liked was the control, the control of me, he was in charge of what happened to me and my body, thinking about it now it's not dissimilar to a pimp I suppose. It wasn't the nicest of feelings. I felt used by the other men, like I was taking one for the team. I was laying there with a cock in my mouth, two in my hands and one fucking me while Simon was encouraging them. We didn't go again.

We'd go out for dinner and he'd have me wear no underwear and discreetly finger me at the table and play with my nipples, which was quite fun, especially after a bottle of wine or two, there was always wine involved.

He encouraged me to actively seek other men for threesomes so I put an ad in a paper, this was a long time ago, there was no internet, but I was inundated and then spent ages trawling through all the applications, all awful apart from one who was absolutely gorgeous. 6'3", tall dark and handsome, a real gorgeous gent, engaged but not allowed premarital sex apparently so looking elsewhere for some NSA (no strings attached). I met him a few times but Simon wasn't interested in a threesome with him as he knew he had the bigger dick. We never did have a threesome there.

I went to a party in a hotel once, it was a girl's birthday and it was her fantasy to be fucked by five or six men. I was only attracted to one of them, a solicitor and I wouldn't play with anyone else. I was at these places giving out sex hoping to find a partner, how flipping ridiculous that seems now. But I never thought I was good enough to have a partner if I didn't offer sex.

It's like the old song 'Why am I always the bridesmaid? Never the blushing bride' the modern version of that is 'Why am I the fuck? Never the girlfriend' and it's obvious now, but at the time I just didn't get it.

When I think back to some of the men I saw there it's so painful. Meeting in a hotel room and bringing their mate along for free sex, horrible, just horrible but I felt so worthless, if I didn't give away sex I'd never get a man's attention surely? I said, "no" a lot too though, if there was no attraction, but it was just the most horrible, horrible time and I thought it was so fun and grown up, how wrong was I. I was screaming inside, someone PLEASE love me, but I didn't know how to attract that, I'd never been good enough for anything or anyone.

The job at the wheat board finished and I moved to the transit authority as a credit controller, much more my cup of tea. I was going to OA in Sydney but my food was still off the wall, did meet some nice people there though. Simon and I finished, he was never going to leave his partner so we parted and I made plans to come back home in June. We did make up before I left and we spent my last night at a hotel on the beach in Coogee. I have a lovely photo of him.

I flew back via LA and travelled down through Mexico to Mexico City on a bus. At that time I wore a gold cross and chain and while I was on the bus a young couple approached me with a baby and wanted me to have the baby for the cross and chain. I was shocked and it broke my heart to think they must be that poor or desperate to need to give up their baby.

From Mexico City I went west to a beach called Zihuatanejo, it's where they end up in 'The Shawshank Redemption' I later realised, got very sunburnt. Stayed a few days and the waiter plied me with Corona and then asked me back to his so I walked along this beautiful beach with a massive full moon beaming down. When we got to his it wasn't a nice place and the cat had shit everywhere, so I left and wandered back. On the way there were some fishermen spit roasting a massive fish, tuna I think. Will never forget that moment, there was just something very special about it, with this beautiful full moon, as I walked along that beach I wanted to stay there forever but how? I travelled back up through the Chihuahua Valley by train, stunning. At some point I visited Jo again in San Francisco again and we went to the cinema to see Jurassic Park that had just been released, it terrified us, how it ever got a PG we will never know.

I also travelled from Singapore up through Malaysia, stopping in Kuala Lumpur, Kota Bharu and going out to the island where they made South Pacific. Another time I went via Koh Pee Pee and Krabbi and then further north to Mah Hon Seng and along the river seeing elephants wallowing to Chiang Rai, all amazing places to see. I am a whistle stop tourist though, I don't hang about, been there, seen it, got the picture... next.

When I returned home Claire was lodging with Caroline, I didn't get it, how come Caroline never ever wanted me to live with her yet Claire did? What's wrong with me?

My cousins were getting married when I got home so there were two weddings within weeks of each other. Speaking to Rachel, my sister's friend at one of them she said, "your Dad is so proud of you". I looked puzzled and she said, "he talks about you constantly, you're the apple of his eye, definitely the favourite". I was shocked, I had absolutely no idea, all we did was argue and I'd spent years screaming obscenities down the phone at him while Mum was in tears over the latest affair. It just didn't make sense to me, him being proud of me, we rarely got on, we just argued constantly.

He always bailed me out financially, but it was Mum who had control of the purse strings in reality. I did always pay them back though. They replaced the engine in my Austin Healey Sprite when I blew it up being raced home by someone along the M4, just about made it to Marshfield. They gave me the card for telephone calls while I went travelling, that was how he showed his love, with money, never a cuddle or a kind word, quite the opposite but all I ever wanted was a cuddle and to be loved, but I never felt I got that, ever.

I didn't have a car when I came back from Australia so I moved in with Andy temporarily who had a small flat on the tenth floor in a block at the Elephant and Castle. I'd lived with him before on Queens Road. I'd dragged him up from Wiltshire to be my assistant in New Covent Garden and then he'd moved to Highbury with us all. He was Kerry's ex-boyfriend but they were now both openly gay, it was fairly obvious he was, so dragging him to London at twentyish was a good move, he's still there.

DREAM JOB

I found a room to rent in a house on Battersea Bridge Road so moved in there with Graham and another guy. I liked Graham, probably a little too much but it was OK living with them, once I'd cleaned the place. I was alone though, and I liked it that way, or so I convinced myself. I would meet Rachel occasionally and her friend Andrea for dinner sometimes. We met three barristers when out for dinner one night, one of them had defended Stephen Fry when he'd disappeared. We were all VERY drunk and when I left to drive home at 4am I set the alarm off on the cars next to mine. I'd often spend my Saturdays and Sundays on the Fulham Road seeing two or three films alone. Sat behind Ian Hislop once, presumably on a date, he didn't stop talking all the way through a film, drove me nuts, so I moved seats. I was still back home in Chippenham a lot on Saturday nights too though.

I got a job in credit control for a business services company in Stockwell which I liked and one Friday I went to the Irish pub opposite Stockwell tube and got very drunk with a colleague. We got chatting to a girl, Alison, and her boyfriend. It was a very packed pub. Alison and I became friends and decided to move in together so we found a lovely flat in Albert Palace Mansions in Battersea. The day we moved in Alison sat really close to me on the sofa and leaned in to kiss me much to my surprise, I declined her advance. Then she told me that I'd kissed her passionately that night in the pub but I had no recollection of it whatsoever and it didn't happen again, for a while.

Alison liked Arab men, she'd lived in Riyadh for a time and so we used to go to Tokyo Joes on Piccadilly, it was £10 to get in and we never had to buy a drink so a bargain. I got so drunk on a New Year's Eve there a guy offered to take me home in his soft top sports car, a Ferrari or Lamborghini or something. He told his friend to stay in the car while he invited himself in, I kicked him straight back out when I realised he wasn't going to marry me. The hangover from that night lasted two or three days, ugh! One time Alison's friend Helen was visiting the UK and so we decided to go there again. We were sitting at the bar and a man started trying to talk to me as usual and then whispered something in my ear which I couldn't hear, so I looked at him and leaned in to hear better and he repeated a little louder, "£300". My face filled with horror, they thought we were prostitutes, no wonder we never had to buy a drink! We weren't Two Fat Slags, they thought we were three!

I'd always wanted to be a Mortgage Advisor, a guy I'd been at college with was one. He always wore nice suits, had a briefcase and drove a nice car so I figured I was good at arithmetic so maybe I could do that job but I never saw it advertised. So when I saw an ad for a Saturday Salesperson for an estate agency I promptly applied and got an interview in Kennington. The interviewer told me that he'd already employed someone but as soon as another position came up he'd be in touch. Within a week or two I had a call at work. "Credit control Nici speaking how can I help you?" I said.

"Well you've got the job when can you start?" the voice said, it was the manager from the Battersea branch of the estate agency. I went in at 9am that Saturday and within an hour he asked me if I wanted a full-time position to which I said, "no, I want to be a mortgage advisor". "I'll get you an interview on Monday," he said, and he did.

I met the head of mortgage services and started with them in October 1993. By January 1994 I had my Financial Planning Certificate and was a mortgage broker covering supposedly two or three branches but once the estate agents realised you were good and worked hard I was all over the place signing people up, so much so that I was in their Top 10 of 250 brokers nationwide within months.

The only reason I wanted to be in the Top 10 of advisors was because you got a good night out with all the other top achievers and that meant a nice meal, all you could drink and a disco, my favourite evening but I do **love** a karaoke too. But of course I'd be so nervous I'd drink before I got there and all evening. Inevitably I ended up snogging the only bloke I had an eye for and giving him a blow job in the toilet once or twice, always the same bloke though, had a girlfriend, was getting married, usual story.

At one of these events a woman I worked with, drunk, who had been a model previously, said to me, "Nici, I'm not gay but if I were you'd be the woman I'd want". That happened with another woman too, in Chippenham, but they were very beautiful women and straight and I was always very surprised.

I loved my job though, helping people get their dream, their own home and I was very good at it. Only because I'm very thorough and not your typical salesman who just wants you to sign here, take the commission and run, like the bloke in the toilet. If I signed someone up they always completed and I signed up a lot of people I saw, my conversion rate was excellent.

I was based in the Tooting branch of the estate agency with Philip, Maura and Otis. One day I took in a video tape that a colleague had given me, can't recall why. Otis was most curious and asked what it was of so I said, "oh it's just a threesome Simon and I filmed, do you want to see it?" "Yeah," he said so I gave it to him. Philip and Maura were horrified and told him all day not to watch it because 'it's personal' and he 'shouldn't', but he took it home to watch. The next day he came in the office so embarrassed, and we all fell about laughing, laughing so much we were crying. He'd called all his mates and got them round to watch this video and it was the Australian Grand Prix. We did laugh, and laugh and laugh, and so did he, eventually.

Tooting was a great place to work. A bus stop was right opposite the shop and one gloriously sunny summer's day a guy standing there just stripped off completely naked, I can still see him now, just couldn't believe it, picked up his clothes and walked off, completely starkers.

Maura was very secretive about her very long-term boyfriend. One day I was sitting at work and the phone went, it was her day off, and this voice said, "hello Nici, this is…," (can't recall his name), what on earth was he doing calling me? but I was SO curious. A few days later he came to the flat. I opened the door and you could have knocked me over with a feather. Maura was 5', he was 6'4" possibly 6'8", I don't know, but tall, very tall, and black, very black, I was flabbergasted and he knew I was and we both laughed, he had a bottle of wine though so I let him in. We had a pleasant evening, we talked and laughed a lot but I didn't fancy him so there was no way, he left somewhat disappointed, didn't even get a snog that I recall.

It still wasn't a happy time in all honesty. I was drinking loads at every opportunity, overeating constantly, dieting, bingeing, starving constantly and crying a lot too, always thinking that one day some man was going to appear and save me. I always had a man in my head, usually the last one I'd snogged, but some when around then I caught something and ended up at the sexual health clinic in Tooting with my legs in stirrups again crying as this old male doctor poked around and muttered something. I was SO humiliated and SO ashamed, whatever it was went very quickly, again.

Although I worked in London I came home a lot at weekends to go out. One Saturday night we were in Chippenham in a nightclub, by this time Goldigger's had shut and there were two much smaller ones in town. As the lights went up I clocked a man on the other side of the room and just thought 'Wow!'. I was drunk, no, never? Yep, drunk, so I went over to him, held out my hand to shake his, which he did, introduced myself, he said his name was Sam, "who are you going home with?" he said, "no-one," so I said, "shall we?" And that was it. We went back to his. I remember making him come without touching his dick, I SO wanted to impress him, he was my kind of gorgeous, very fit, jeans and tight white t-shirt, cropped hair, nice cheek bones, just something about him I was really attracted to physically and as we talked I liked him more. He was single too, but eight or ten years younger than me, not that I cared at all. I came home a few weeks running to accidentally on purpose bump into him but for him it was always just for the sex, he never asked me out and after three or four weeks he was on to the next one. Bobby Brown's '*Two can play that game*' continues to remind me of him, he's a great dancer.

At Christmas I went to Delhi, travelled north to Amritsar then through Nepal to Kathmandu, saw the sun rise over the Ganges at Varanasi, went down to Calcutta, west to Bombay and then to Goa to spend Christmas with the motorway lot who had frequented the wine bar I'd run for a while. I travelled alone, always alone, I'd like to say I preferred it that way, and I did, but the truth is I never have friends who want to come anywhere with me. There were no men, ever, when I travelled. I did quite like a Welsh guy I met in Goa but nothing happened, he was tall, big, dark haired, a bit Tom Jones I suppose, do love a Welsh accent, love most accents.

I came home and the estate agency had a big presentation evening at the Palladium. They'd asked all the top producers to be in a video film that they wanted to show at this presentation, I wasn't happy about it, I'm 15 stone, can't bear to even look at myself and they want me on film? But I had to do it, so I did, it was just a brief interview with each of us. The night of this presentation came, everyone was really excited about getting dressed up, I hated getting dressed up, how can I look nice? So I drank while I was getting ready. Maura picked me up in a taxi and I was drunk then. We were late getting there and thank heavens we were, my bit in the film was last on and we missed it, I just couldn't have coped with seeing myself on a huge screen. I don't remember the evening at all, don't think I gave anyone a blow job in the toilet but I did get a lift home with my bosses boss and the MD whose lap I sat on the whole way and whose face I snogged off, poor, poor man, I am sorry.

A guy who befriended the motorway lot while in India lived in London and was in touch so one weekend I drove him to Chippenham as a surprise for them. It was a nice weekend which he enjoyed. That Friday night I stayed at Jerry's which was always very casual and comfortable. On Saturday night I ended up with the only motorway guy I did fancy a bit but was really disappointed for the usual reason, heavens only knows how that happened, why ever would he sleep with me? I was fat and ugly and he always had very pretty girlfriends but I suppose sex is a lure. He seemed to want to be with me the next night too but I just couldn't understand it, why did he ever want to see me again? Most odd, no one ever comes back, so I went off with another guy I'd fancied for years who happened to be around that evening, who never came back either.

After a year or so I decided I'd move back home if I could find a job, and I did, quickly, with a local estate agency but the current lot didn't want me to leave so got me a transfer which I stuck for six months and then I moved.

I walked into the Chippenham branch of the new company for an interview with this 6'3" red haired rugby player who was going to be my manager, he looked me up and down and said, "you must be Nici, let's go out the back". As soon as we sat down in the back office he said, "do you want to come skiing next week?" So I laughed and wished with all my heart that I could ski, but I can't and never have, so I said, "no thank you". I got the job.

I fancied every inch of him, within weeks we were having sex in the kitchens of the offices where he had to observe me, in his office in Bristol and at his mates flat. If we could, we did, he was gorgeous, and married with a baby on the way. Bjork's '*It's oh so quiet*' is the record that still reminds me of him. But of course, it was another affair and I was never good enough and the evening that he was flirting with his next conquest broke my heart so I fled home and sobbed. That sobbing when the snot is pouring out of my nose again. I awoke the next morning with my eyelids and sockets bright red and puffed up and my eyes bloodshot and tiny little slits because they're so swollen from the pain of the tears, and the heartache, the heartache of being used, again.

And so in retaliation I slept with his friend and then a manager from a branch within weeks, that'd show him, not. And of course, they weren't interested in me either, it was just sex after all, no strings, just sex. But that's such a lie. I've never enjoyed sex like that, I loved the kissing and the skin next to skin but I was just whoring it, desperate to be loved, desperate for someone to accept me, like me, want me.

Simon came over from Australia and I went to London to meet him to go to a Soho strip club, because I was curious and had never been, so I wanted to go and see what one was like. Rather dull really, don't know what I was expecting, it was small and seedy. I didn't like it so we left after one drink and went to meet a friend of his from Oz who was over and game for a threesome. Plenty of drinking ensued, for me at least, and we got a black cab back to the hotel, I was almost naked in the back of this cab with Simon and his friend all over me. We arrived at this friend's hotel room, I was expecting an amazing evening and was gutted when I realised the guy only had an acorn dick. Another control tactic by Simon, to ensure he was top dog, made his very average penis seem plentiful, although he was very good with fingers and tongue, as some men are. In my experience men with a more modest penis often try a lot harder to please than those rather more well-endowed.

Now I was living back in Chippenham. I moved in with Claire and Will, her boyfriend, on Malmesbury Road, which was really nice, Claire and I were close again, we'd sit up and chat most nights but after a couple of weeks she asked me to leave because it wasn't working out. Will didn't like us being close I'm sure. I found another room to rent in Chippenham with a girl I knew so it was fine. I was back to going out in Chippenham on Friday and Saturday nights, getting very drunk. I had two girlfriends, Heidi and Mia, who could drink as much as me, so I thought, it was a raucous time. I worked very hard and played harder. But what I could never understand was that if I slept with a man they never came back. Yet whenever Claire or Caroline slept with one they always seemed to come back, they always became, or wanted to become, the next boyfriend, but it never worked like that for me, ever.

One of these girlfriends had children and I loved taking them out. I piled as many children as I could in my car and took them all off to see Casper in Swindon. I'd often take them out to parks or babysit but never charge, just wanted to give them some attention and love, and have a bit of quiet me time if possible, write my diary or watch a film. Once though I promised to take one of them out but had such a raging hangover I was still in bed when she eventually got hold of me, I felt so awful for letting her down, just awful, the sadness in her beautiful little face pained me when I next saw her, it reminded me of myself.

Caroline and I arranged to go out one night together in Chippenham but she called to say she couldn't make it, she wasn't feeling like going out so could we give it a miss, so I said, "yeah that's OK," and called another friend and went out with her instead. When we were out that night Caroline was out with other friends, I was heartbroken, what on earth is wrong with me? Why don't people like me? Why don't people want to be with me? Why does everybody hate me? Why's it all my fault? The old record just kept on playing.

A friend had a girls' night in one evening, there were a few of us, and I got very drunk, can you see the pattern? We made a list of the men I'd had sex with which we all found hilarious, we got up to sixty or so. I'd had sex with, certainly hadn't slept with, sixty or so men and almost every one of them I'd wanted to be a boyfriend and of course none of them ever had become my boyfriend. And I thought this was hilarious, yeah, really hilarious.

Alison came to visit me in Chippenham and we went out and got very drunk, again. After a day of drinking we went home and slept together. I had had sex with women in Australia, only very briefly, during a threesome, but this was something else and a one off. A woman knows what a woman wants, and top of that list is no snakes or poker tongues when kissing and some men do that and it's horrible, DON'T! Gentle, sensual, soft, it's always about the kiss, if that ain't good we're off to a bad start, believe me.

The girl I was lodging with got a boyfriend, I had to move out and so I moved back to Mum and Dad's. It was time to buy a house, I was a mortgage broker after all. I bought my first house on Downing Street in Chippenham for £39,000 and got the keys on January 12th 1996. Good things always happen around January 12th, it was Nan's birthday. I couldn't move in, it needed totally gutting but I relished that challenge and got stuck in straight away, I do love a project. It was a three-bed Victorian terrace just like the ones I loved in London, though soon to be a two-bed with bathroom upstairs.

ALEX

One night in late May we were out, by this time Heidi had a house and a boyfriend, but we still all went out together as he was in the army, with her brother which is how they'd met years before they got together. Why didn't I have a brother like that, mind you I fancied Darrell, Heidi's brother but he wasn't interested in me. This night there'd been a big football match on and lots of drunk men were about, one of which was the attractive, quiet one, Alex, that I'd always noticed when I was hounding Pete. I spoke to him and he bought me a drink, we danced, a smooch (he can't dance) and then sat and talked for ages. We were the same age, he was at the boys' school, while I was at the girls', we knew lots of the same people so had lots to talk about. We kissed and then we went home to Heidi's with her and Joe. We had to listen to their rampant drunken love making while we cuddled up and talked and... yes. He had all the right equipment but wasn't particularly good at using it. I soon got it all working to my liking though.

I dropped him off the next day and that was it, end of. But it wasn't. A few weeks later we bumped into each other again, I was really hoping we would. That night my sister was away and I knew where the key was so we slept in their spare room. He asked for my number and when he called I was happy, really happy, someone had come back. He lived in Gloucestershire with his in-laws, not that he'd ever married, but he had a six year old son and when his partner left he said he couldn't leave his son too and I liked that, that he'd stayed for his son.

They say, don't they, (who are they?) that if you put a ball in a bag every time you have sex in the first year together it'll take you twenty-five years to take those balls out each time you have sex thereafter. Suffice to say there was a lot of sex, otherwise he wouldn't want me would he? I am a performer when it comes to sex, I swing from chandeliers, why would any man want me in their life otherwise? I have to do something extraordinary to make a man stay don't I? No one would ever like me for me surely, would they?

Simon came over from Australia again and we met and went for a drink and he'd arranged for us to stay at his sisters who was away, but when we got to bed I burst into tears because I knew I wanted to be with Alex. Simon was very understanding and kind, and pleased for me, but slightly disappointed too he said.

I only had the bedroom and bathroom finished in Downing Street but I wanted to move in, so a fridge with a microwave on top would do for a kitchen temporarily and it did. For my birthday Alex bought me a tap and a back door, the ones I chose, and the house got finished and I absolutely loved it. I needed a lodger so he had to decide, he moved in or I got a lodger. On August bank holiday weekend there we were, in Ikea, buying a double bed, felt so weird being with someone, but so nice too.

Channel 4 came knocking one day, doing a TV programme about the election and would we be interested in coming along to the studio with other people from Downing Street in Glasgow to be in the audience for a politics programme, can't recall the damn name know, the older man that presented it has since died. It was a good day out though and we stopped for dinner on the way home in Chelsea. Alex was a Chelsea season ticket holder so we were often in London which I liked, bought my sofa on the Kings Road.

I spent far too much on him at Christmas, buying a leather jacket and numerous other gifts, always on credit card. I always spent more money than I earned, the bank had more money than me so I might as well use theirs. I thought nothing about debts and always just spent money as and when I wanted to, regardless of income.

I did struggle with being in a relationship. I liked the company but couldn't bear it somehow too. I could scream and shout a lot and in the next breath be very loving and kind, just unable to cope with what I'd always wanted, being loved.

For Alex's birthday in March we saw Jimmy Nail in Birmingham on his Crocodile Shoes tour and stayed in a four-star hotel and then we went to Paris on EuroStar, all a surprise, he knew nothing about any of it. We spent a few days in Paris and it was lovely. I'd never travelled with anyone before and it was so nice to share that experience together. We bought expensive Gucci and Rayban sunglasses on the Champs Elysees. It was quite magical, Paris is lovely. Everything went on a credit card, always.

A couple of weeks later I got cystitis, something Claire suffered with but not me. I got some stuff from Boots and took it and then, a few days later, realised I was pregnant. Claire and Will had been trying for ages, it seemed so unfair.

I couldn't believe it, all that time I'd longed to be pregnant by Pete and never was. I thought that my termination had thwarted my chances of ever having a baby, and Alex having Victor meant I didn't need my own child. Relations with the ex in-laws and his ex were difficult because Victor was loving being with us, so much so he stood in front of his mother one day a few months after we'd met and said, "I love Nici not you", which didn't go down very well. I did love having him though. I've always loved children, not babies so much, they didn't seem to like me, I always thought it was because I have a deep voice, which I blamed on my time in New Covent Garden market, the cold air must have made my voice deep and babies don't like it, probably complete rubbish.

It wasn't an easy time. Alex didn't want another child but I knew I couldn't get rid of another, this had happened for a reason, something greater than me had made this happen and I had to go with it, no way was I going through that pain for all those years again. I was determined that this baby would be a part of my life but wouldn't change it, so even though my taste buds changed and I didn't like the taste I continued to drink six to eight pints of Stella a night in the pub. It was a standing joke that if the baby was a girl I'd have to call her Stella.

I sold Downing Street and we moved to a three-bed detached on Ryan Avenue. All the money I made on Downing Street just about covered what I'd spent on doing it up and overspending, so we had as much mortgage as possible again.

On 16th December 1997, Ben arrived, at 4lbs 12oz, by emergency caesarean in the RUH, Bath. I chose to get off the planet but they did wake me up to glance at him. He was, still is, the most beautiful precious man on this earth to me and it is still, and always will be, one of the most amazing and happiest days of my life.

I had a few weeks off on maternity leave but the day I put the TV on I decided it was time to go back to work, Ben was about six weeks old and he went to my cousin's wife who was a child minder. I lost all my weight when I had Ben, it just fell off of me.

I called Alex at work one day in April '98 and said, "What are you doing on 23rd May?" "Well the FA cup is the week before and the World Cup is the week after so probably nothing much". "We're getting married," I told him and we did. Ben was my bouquet and we had him Christened too in Castle Combe church with a reception at Grittleton House for seventy people and a hundred or so more in the evening.

I had a long ivory straight skirt with a split on one leg and a dark blue velvet off the shoulder tight bodice. I was going to have a flower thing in my hair but when it arrived it looked like a sanitary towel so I called the hat shop in Devizes and my friend picked up a hat I'd ordered to wear the following week for Kerry's commitment ceremony to Jane. It was just like the one Andie MacDowell wore in Four Weddings, looked great, thank goodness.

When I returned to work I had a new boss who I thought didn't like me, I always thought people didn't like me. I didn't like him too much because of this so I decided to leave and was out of there around August '98 to become self-employed.

The money stopped coming in and things got very tight, especially after spending £23k on a cheap wedding. I was still spending like a lunatic, holidays in the main, they just allowed me to drink from 11am, any excuse. I only drank in the evenings apart from weekends if there was football on or we went out for lunch, which I'd often organise. I wasn't into designer this and that because I never felt I looked nice so my money didn't go on clothes very much. I don't like having clothes I don't wear, I do like to wear stuff out.

We moved from the three bed detached to a three bed semi around the corner and cleared some debts, I'd been robbing Pete to pay Paul for ages and the credit cards were going through the roof as I had barely any income.

We went all over Europe watching Chelsea, staying in nice hotels, any excuse to drink a bit more was good by me, all on credit card.

I was approached by an insurance company to work for them so I joined and had to go on a course in Swindon. I got very drunk in the evenings and slept with a massive good looking body builder bloke with a tiny penis, never my favourite experience, but I was crazy enough to want him for a little while, thank goodness it wasn't for long. I never thought there was anything wrong with sleeping with someone else, it just felt normal to me, monogamy is dull, I preferred the rollercoaster of infidelity.

I didn't last long with the insurance company either, I'm not a salesperson, despite what people think. I always advised my clients the same I would advise my children.

I'd kept in touch with Lawri who always had a new idea for a business and the latest one was an insurance discount company. I visited him in Cardiff one day and looked at some mortgage leads he had on his desk but couldn't deal with. I asked if I could call them and within minutes I had two or three potential sign ups so that was it, I went to work for him on a self-employed basis. I realised quickly though that I was doing all the work and he was doing very little so I registered to start my own company and did so some months later.

I suffered with bad psoriasis on my forehead and through my scalp at this time and the skin on my face started to get bumpy and red so I stopped drinking lager, seemed to do the trick, white or pink wine didn't seem to have the same effect so I could drink that.

Alex was still working as a warehouseman doing nights and I would drink every evening, at least a bottle of wine, the white or pink stuff.

Ben wouldn't go to bed and would cry until I took him from his room into my bed, anything for an easy life and another drink.

I'd met someone on the course with the insurance company who'd lost their son of 21 to alcoholism and told me I should have another baby because you never know what life holds so I told Alex I wanted another baby but he wasn't going to have another so I decided, "OK, no sex". Three weeks later on holiday for Alex's birthday in Rimini I fell pregnant.

This time I did stay off of the drink, only had the odd glass here and there and I don't think I enjoyed them, taste buds just go weird when I'm pregnant.

I missed the window to have a nuchal translucency to test for Downs syndrome so I decided to have an amniocentesis privately at which the doctor asked if I'd like to know the sex of the baby, "no thank you". A few days later we received the letter saying the test was normal with the sex of the baby tippexed out, it had six letters, I went numb with fear. Oh my god, she might be just like me, I don't want someone, anyone, especially a daughter to be like me. I mourned for a week, trying to console myself that it would be OK, I was having a daughter, it would all be OK, her life wouldn't be like mine, and it isn't.

We holidayed in Rome when I was six months pregnant, for my birthday, and lots of old women would come up and bless my tummy, most peculiar but sweet.

My business was slowly increasing solely with referrals and I started to earn more and more. After a year or so funds were better so I wanted to move to a four bed detached, on Pewsham this time, as it was a bit cheaper that end of town and I just love moving and having a project.

Nadia was born naturally on December 18th, 2000, another best day of my life moment. She was, is, the most beautiful and precious person in my life, along with Ben. Childbirth is amazing. The pains started like the mildest period pain I'd ever had and ended as the worst I'd ever had. I didn't seem to dilate for ages. I literally crawled into the RUH on my hands and knees to get my face on the floor, because the floor was cold and that was what I wanted, to be cool, I seemed to be boiling. A couple of hours later when I asked for an epidural, I was 8cm dilated or something and the midwife said, "oh my dear, far too late for that, she'll be here in twenty minutes," and she was. The most perfect beautiful daughter I could ever have imagined or dreamed of and she still is, absolutely perfect.

For my thirty-ninth birthday we were going to go to New York but at the last minute I decided Barcelona was a better idea and perhaps for my fortieth we'd go to New York. So at 9.30am on September 11th 2001 we arrived at our hotel in Barcelona to see the twin towers in flames on the TV screen behind the reception area in the hotel. We would have been flying into New York at that very moment if I hadn't have changed my mind at the last minute.

It happened again later too, we had flights booked to go to Assisi but Alex professed we couldn't afford to go so reluctantly I listened to him, that was probably a first, and we didn't go. A few days later there was an earthquake there and a school collapsed killing children inside that I recall, dreadful, absolutely dreadful, incredibly sad.

Ben and I were shopping one day and bumped into a little girl he was at nursery with and her mum at the checkout. I knew the mum vaguely, she'd been in Goa when I was there, and her daughter commented something about another mum, comparing me to her and then added, "but she's not pretty like you". I was shocked, that was the first time, ever, in my life, I'd been called pretty. I did have a man stop me in on Clapham High Street once, just stood right in front of me and said, "You are beautiful". And I worked in Lakota in Bristol for a little while, couldn't stand the music so I didn't stay long, but a guy told the person I was working with "Can you tell your colleague she's the most beautiful woman I've ever seen", clearly off their heads, both of them.

All the time Ben and Nadia were growing up I would often think of my mother and think how could you have been SO cruel, SO cruel. I did ask her one day, "do you love me?" to which she replied, "I fed, clothed and watered you didn't I". What did my mother teach me? Not to lie for one, and that the three biggest lies in the world are:

1) My cheque is in the post
2) My wife doesn't understand me
3) I promise I won't come in your mouth.

And subconsciously that the bank has more money than me, so use theirs and so long as a man sleeps in your bed what they get up to elsewhere is OK. She also despised women that had affairs with married or attached men. When women had an affair and it was publicised my mother would duly chastise them regularly. She had to berate the women who had the affairs, especially the ones Dad had affairs with because they had to be the problem, it was the women that were the problem, not Dad, it couldn't possibly be her, or their relationship that was at fault could it? Possibly?

23rd May 1998

BOOM AND BUST

Business was booming, income was increasing and I had to take on a part time admin assistant to help me. Both Ben and Nadia were full time at nursery. I thought I could work from home with Nadia as a newborn but it seemed that every time the phone rang she'd cry and I'd just have to listen to her, which I couldn't bear, so after a week or two she was the youngest full time baby at the nursery.

We had lots of holidays, three or more a year, all enabling me to drink more. When we weren't on holiday we would eat out a lot and spend weekends in pubs with children's play areas or football on big screens. On a sunny afternoon in the Pack Horse one day there were a lot of people drinking together, not that I ever felt I was one of them or that I was in the gang or crowd. I was berating Alex as usual, I would always put him down and ridicule and belittle him in front of people about how useless he was but I didn't realise I was doing it until Caroline pulled me up on it, made me think, and I never did it again, that I'm aware of. I realised years later too that my mother does the same with my father, constantly, saying how useless he is, no doubt she learnt it from her mother too, horrible, just horrible. When I'm criticising, chastising, belittling and ridiculing someone else I suppose, subconsciously, I feel powerful, what I'm actually doing is showing how insecure and self-loathing I am of me.

I advertised at Chippenham Football Club and sometimes sponsored the match so we would go and invite friends along for drinks in the corporate hospitality lounge which was a prefab. Watching the match one day there were some large houses being built on old school land, so we bought one. I needed an office big enough for two people at least and this house had that, far better to increase the mortgage than rent something and I didn't have any pension provision. I'd rather invest in my own property than give an investment company my hard-earned cash.

By this time Alex had given up work and was a house husband doing my accounts, playing golf and I really don't know what else because I seemed to do a lot of the other stuff and we had a cleaner and a gardener and mum did the laundry for me.

We moved in to our five bed detached with four bathrooms in Portal Close on February 14th 2003 we didn't get any welcome to your new home cards, I only mention it because I remember seeing other people with lots of them on their window sills. It cost £385k and Alex always said it would bankrupt us but I wanted it and it was only money after all, the bank had more than us so why not use theirs?

I spent a small fortune buying all the furniture, soft furnishings, pictures and bits and pieces that I needed to make it my perfect home, the home we barely used four rooms in but it all looked really good. I couldn't find pictures big enough for my liking, or the right colours, so I bought canvas the right size and got tester pots of the colours I wanted and threw the paints at the canvas then swirled them about a bit with a kitchen brush and various other implements and hung them in my sitting room and they looked fabulous, just what I wanted, contemporary art by ns.

Alex had friends from his old Sunday football team and we'd have poker nights with all the partners which was fun, did love poker. I had an Anne Summers party one evening, all the women on the close came and a few others and we drank, quite a lot, or I did. One of the women commented on my artwork and asked where I'd got it from "oh that little gallery behind Jollys in Bath," I said. An hour or so later they were surprised when I told them I'd done them myself and wouldn't believe me until I pointed out the signature ns, my initials.

When the hostess gave me my commission at the end of the evening she told me it had been her best party ever for sales. I bought nipple clamps with the proceeds and immediately put them on, bit too painful though, needed adjustment, a few of us tried them, never used them again. Perhaps the others were a bit drunk.

We also had a summer party in September, invited the whole close and guests, nice party, friends band played on the lawn, had clay pigeon shooting going on, barbeque, it was a nice evening. I also gave Will and Claire an invite, we'd not spoken for years after some falling out, again, for a year or three and they came to the party. Probably just being nosey because we had the big house but it was all hugs and kisses and all was fine, again, until the next time.

Alex pointed out to me one day "do you know you haven't moved from that chair since 8am this morning", it was 10pm. I got too busy to work from home and so did end up renting a shop in town in 2004 and by then had an almost full-time admin person. We continued going on lots of holidays and eating out most evenings, business was booming, so I took an ad on local commercial radio too. We expected the phone to ring immediately that the ad ran but of course it didn't. All the ad did was get my name out there so when my name was mentioned thereafter people said they knew it. I'm not sure if it got me business, it got me notoriety, I was world famous in Chippenham.

Around May 2004 we'd been out with Mum and Dad for lunch one Sunday and something was said and I blew, told them to get out and never come back and that was it, we've barely spoken since, best thing I ever did which seems harsh but the reason will reveal itself as we go on. I haven't spoken to my sisters since then either.

Our neighbour was forty and her husband organised a surprise party in the Bear in Chippenham and then we all went to the club where Alex and I had met but he went home and I stayed out with an old girl-friend. I always drank a lot when I was out in company, it hid my nerves and took away my belief that everybody hated me, especially around my neighbours, after all I was the only main earner working woman on this new estate. I did feel uncomfortable though despite drinking and so when an ex of Caroline's turned up, who I'd always fancied, it seemed like a really good idea to sit on his lap and completely snog his face off in front of all my neighbours, that'd show them, though what it showed them I have no idea, just that I could be a slag I suppose, I just wanted to upset their perfect applecarts. I also got rather amorous with another neighbour and told him I'd, "have him," one day. 6'+ and red haired, always seem to be attracted to those men.

Brent and I left the party, I could barely stand up but we were going back to his. When we arrived his girlfriend was home so we walked over the road to the graveyard. It was a beautiful full moon lit night and we had sex amongst the graves, like you do when you're, no, like I do, when I'm completely plastered and snogging a bloke I've fancied for many, many years who chose to go out with the friend I'd introduced him to and not me, now it was my turn, at last.

I staggered home and crawled into bed. I stayed there almost all day, as usual, with a raging hangover and got up about 5pm, as usual, to go out for dinner with Alex and the children and start drinking all over again.

The next morning I was consumed with guilt, or was I? The alarm went off and the radio came on so I turned to Alex and said, "I've got to tell you something." As I did Leanne Rhymes 'How do I live without you' came on the radio, that's Alex's song for me, I couldn't believe it. I told him what I'd done and with who, he was a friend of ours, and said, "I'm not going anywhere, if you want to leave that's up to you, but I'm not," to which he replied, "will it happen again?", "I don't know and can't promise that," I said.

Being honest I was never comfortable with Alex telling me that 'How do I live without you' was his song for me, I found it really too much, sickly. It bothered me.

Out another night in Chippenham I bumped into Sam, I've always got the hots for that man, I'm not sure why, I just find him incredibly attractive, and so we arranged to meet later on. I was so drunk when I danced later I fell flat on my face. I got a cab home and as I walked in he sent a text, "where are you?" which I quickly deleted along with his number.

I decided Alex and I should go to Relate, for marriage counselling. We went for one session and it was very apparent it was my problem and not Alex's. I did divulge to him in that session that I felt masses of guilt about the number of men I'd slept with but he didn't flinch. That night I drank more than usual. When we got to bed I wanted consoling but Alex was never supportive like that. I just wanted a cuddle and to be loved but it wasn't there so I went downstairs, sobbing, you know, when the snot is pouring from your nose sobbing, sobbing like the grieving session in rehab, again, so I called the Samaritans. I spent three hours on the phone to them, sobbing, pouring my heart out about the guilt I felt for sleeping with loads of men, the guilt from the termination and very, very slowly it was like some great weight was lifted from me, not immediately, but over the coming weeks and possibly years.

Alex didn't come to another Relate session, he was OK, it was me that had the problem. Over the next few months I had a few light bulb moments during the counselling, for instance Mum always gets close to the man that's closest to me because I won't let her near me. And that the reason I left home and went back time and time again in my twenties and early thirties was because I was trying to get the love I never had, it was never there, never will be. I did ask Mum one day, when we were speaking, it never lasts long, if she loved me, she said "of course I love you, you're my daughter, I don't like you very much sometimes though".

I was drinking a bottle of wine almost every evening by now, plus whatever I'd drunk when we were out, usually another bottle. I was 15-16 stone, size 22 top and 18 bottom, not sleeping very well, would wake or not sleep because of hot flushes but couldn't for the life of me think what it was that was keeping me awake. I wonder what it could have been?

I fell pregnant and six weeks later I lost it, heart breaking. I caught the foetus in my hand as it fell from me, I called Ben, he's never forgotten seeing it. My heart ached and the tears rolled down my face.

Business continued to boom, I continued to drink too much, spend too much, eat too much, life rumbled on. I was continuing with therapy, trying to sort out what was wrong with me, as usual, because there obviously was something very wrong with me, everyone else was fine, it was just me that was the problem.

Simon would call from Australia while I was in the shop quite regularly and we'd talk and talk and I'd fantasise about how it would so wonderful to be with him and then he came over for his sixtieth and I took one look at him and didn't want him at all, after all those years of thinking I did.

Nadia was diagnosed with Ulcerative Colitis in 2006, which was horrendous. Bleeding lumps like pieces of liver from her bottom and screaming in pain with her legs curled up to her chest, crying, just awful, especially if she ate something strong in flavour, a Pepperami or even a ready meal macaroni cheese once.

I feel dreadfully guilty saying that because I'm quite a good cook, my children disagree with that statement, but as I worked more and more and Alex was at home with the children he would give them frozen food all the time when we didn't eat out. I hated it but was more intent on earning money than feeding my children healthily. The nursery had said that Ben was the only child that ate vegetables, but when he got to primary school a little boy said, "er what you eating that for," and Ben has never touched a vegetable since, the closest he gets even now is tomato ketchup and the odd portion of peas, hardly adequate. I still to this day disguise onion, celery and carrot in any bolognese sauce but he does eat that, probably won't if he reads this, but they both insist they will never read this. Nadia is slightly better and will eat fruit and vegetables but not very often, mostly it's carbs and they're going to live to regret it, it's all refined sugar, even flour is too.

As a mum I felt so much guilt when Nadia was ill, it must be my fault, of course it's my fault, everything is always my fault, I've done something terribly wrong, that's why she's got this. Of course at the time the doctors had no explanation as to why she had it but put her on steroids which made her as high as a kite and bloated her cheeks like a squirrel with a mouth full of nuts.

At the same time we'd been to the dentist and she'd had to have a filling. She'd just started to drink Coke so we reduced that and her sweet intake that she got given by Grandma and Nanny and guess what, the UC settled. So much so that I weaned her off of the medication, I can't see the point in taking something permanently, surely when you need it it won't be so effective? Anyway, I mentioned this to my doctor who just looked at his feet, as usual, but when I told the consultant she wasn't happy and said, "well I won't see you again then". So we left on the understanding that if there was a flare up we would get back in touch, that was 2008. We've not had any reoccurrences whatsoever. Nadia is aware she has it, sometimes, but very, very rarely and they told us she'd have it for life? I happened to read 'Pure White and Deadly' by John Yudkin because of my sugar addiction. He confirms it's sugar related, I completely agree.

Business was still booming, I was earning £175kpa and spending more. We'd have five or six holidays a year enabling me to drink, I rarely got drunk, drink was just my way to feel normal now. On Thursday evenings I'd work late and meet my window cleaner who I'd become friendly with since opening the shop, he was a friend of Mike's and I liked their company, much more fun than Alex. We'd get very drunk and I'd have a raging hangover all of Friday in the office and would start again around 6pm with Alex and the children in tow.

I had new clients often, all referrals, and one day a very handsome younger man turned up with his fiancé. I arranged their mortgage and sometime after they split up so he came back for another mortgage and we became friends.

I developed a back problem, probably because I sat on a chair and didn't move for 8-10hours, or was it my GG boobs? Who knows? One Sunday morning I just couldn't move for the pain in my lower back. The next day I went to see a chiropractor who did his thing and I walked away in a little less discomfort and went back to work. I continued to see the chiropractor for months, costing a small fortune. He had two springer spaniels who would sit in his office so I asked if walking might help my problem as I used to have a dog, and of course it would so we got Luca, a red setter puppy. I would walk him to the office through the park. I realised I felt good for doing that bit of exercise so added on thirty minutes on the cross trainer at the leisure centre which was in the park, I was nearing forty-five, I needed to get a bit fitter. So the cross trainer slowly increased to an hour and then I tried swimming. Oh my god, that is SO hard, but I started with eight lengths for a week, then sixteen, then twenty-four until after a month or so I was swimming a mile in thirty-five minutes, not too bad. It killed me, still does, but the slight mood lift I get is priceless. Walking Luca daily fixed my lower back problem, never had it since. Best natural anti-depressant known to man, exercise.

I used to go into the office every day and have a pile of client files on my desk that needed to remortgage that month, it was the bread and butter of my business. Business, I didn't own a business I owned my job, if I walked away there was no business, it was me, I owned my job, not a business.

On April 6th 2008 I sat down to place another twenty or so mortgages as usual and got decline, decline, decline. That was it, the bust that we'd been hearing about in the US had hit us, hard, and the mortgage industry was the first to suffer. At first I thought I'd probably earn half of what I'd been earning, then a quarter, then it was less, and less, and less until after a week or three I decided we'd better sell the house. Our mortgage was £2k a month. And let go of the shop, and after a while I thought if I was doing all that I might as well have a clean sweep and get rid of Alex too.

We sold the house in July and moved into the people who bought ours old house on Park Avenue that they wanted to rent out. We were left with £75k or so on cards and loans, we did clear the mortgage though. Alex got a job back in a warehouse, thank goodness, I couldn't be working at home with him there all day. Then I worked out that I could just about survive on my own if I moved him out to a flat, so I did. I told the children that we'd be better off, we weren't sleeping together anyway. We'd bought a queen size bed years before and the children slept with us so moving him in to the spare room was easy, however reluctant he was and the children loved sleeping with me, as I did them.

He didn't want to move out, but I couldn't bear it, him being so close and that damn Leanne Rhymes song haunted me, I couldn't understand that level of infatuation or love, it scared me shitless. I just didn't want him anymore, I preferred a drink, much easier.

Alex continued to come home every evening for dinner and would stay until 8 or 9pm and then go to his flat just down the road. We went on holiday, putting one last extravagance on the credit card, and I slept with the children. He did approach the bed one night but I told him to go away, the pain in his face did make me sad. It was a lovely holiday though, an all-inclusive 4-star place in Turkey. They'd give free wine at mealtimes, so I'd decant a bottle discreetly and take it away for the afternoon and evening to avoid paying their ridiculous prices. We always took games for the children to play on holiday, Uno, Jenga, Dominoes, all so that we could sit there for hours so that I could drink more, on every holiday and there had been many.

We declared ourselves bankrupt in 2009 for £75k, another shameful moment that became one of the best things I ever did. I had to learn to manage my money, I'd never done that, I'd always used the banks as they had more than me. Not being able to get credit was a blessing, a massive blessing, really hard sometimes but such a blessing. There are after all, no credit cards, there are only debt cards. Some months later, sitting in the garden of the George at Lacock, we made a list of all the places we'd been in the thirteen years we'd been together, there were six or seven trips a year, probably costing about £75k in total.

Me on one of our many holidays, note the wine cooler!

INTERNET DATING

Alex always thought he was going to get back in my bed and so the only way I thought I could make him understand that he wasn't going to was to perhaps get someone else in it. My neighbour was a prolific internet dater, had been for years, and still single, but that didn't deter me. I asked him what was the number one rule I should adhere to? He advised me to always ask how old the picture is and that there was no point in paying for it, he'd been on all the sites and the free one was and as good as any of them, this was 2010.

I got Nadia to take an OK picture, because I have none, and duly set up a profile. That evening Alex sat with the children while I went out, heavens knows who with or what for, but it definitely wasn't for a date.

The next morning while I was checking on eBay for what I was selling, we had a lot to sell moving from a large five bed to a smaller semi, a picture of an old lady kept appearing on my screen which I couldn't figure out. When Alex turned up for lunch I mentioned it and he laughed, he'd swopped my picture for the old lady saying, "you'll get loads of hits with that other photo, I'm not having that," still clinging on to the fantasy that we would get back together one day.

The trick backfired on him though. I got very few hits with my pic, but lots with the old lady so I went back to each of them saying, "sorry, my ex babysat and swopped my picture, thanks for your interest but no thanks," they weren't my cup of tea, bar one. I chatted to this guy online for a week or so and realised after a few days that he knew how to play this game so I told him to go away, I wasn't after a player. A week or so later, after a couple of cups of coffee with dull unfit men I went back to him and said, "ok, so how do we play?", I was bored, let's just skip to the best bit.

I met him, on January 12th, often a good day, thank you Nan, albeit very briefly, in a motorway services car park, not Leigh Delamere, very romantic. He'd said he wasn't suitably dressed as he'd just been to the gym but I didn't care about that, I knew that if he passed the three second test all would be OK. The three second test being if I look at you for three seconds and am happy to continue doing so we're good to go, basically I have to fancy you and want your trousers off. As I drove into the car park he was walking to his car, done deal, fancied him, red hair, attractive to me, very fit, cheeky, sold. We chatted in the car for twenty minutes, he put his hand on my knee and said, "you're alright," smiling,

I asked what he meant and he told me, "you wouldn't believe how many woman put old photos on there and are four stone heavier when you meet them," men do the same. He was in a long-term relationship but didn't live with her so could get away and was self-employed too so flexible. I didn't care that he was attached, this was just some NSA after all. I just wanted Alex to get the message loud and clear. We kissed and parted. Nice kiss.

My neighbour was right, always ask the age of the picture and nowadays I'd be asking for full length (without filters) as face selfies hide a multitude of sins.

A week later, after chatting more online daily Harry turned up at my house while the children were at school. He knew how to use his very adequate equipment, knew all the right moves, it was so refreshing to have someone dominant and adventurous, I was in heaven, for all of three hours because he was a master, could come three or four times in an afternoon, thank god for batteries. For many years I've had a bullet, still have it but very rarely, if ever, use it now, in fact I gave the women who worked for me one for their birthdays. It just speeds up the orgasm, otherwise I'd be ages waiting for one, can't be bothered with that anymore, I need to be in love for that stuff, sadly that isn't happening.

I continued to look and was enticed by other dating sites that would ping up, so and so is interested in you, and of course it's hugely flattering to receive this stuff so I paid to join another site and as soon as I did the guy mentioned disappeared into thin air. I'm convinced there's a warehouse somewhere, or maybe it's done from home? Where women, and men perhaps, just sit and chat to the opposite sex, probably for minimum wage, to keep people paying subscriptions. Actually, I bet it's done by a computer now they're so clever, much cheaper than minimum wage.

I discovered I'm really not very good at the chit chat, I decided on 'meet me or delete me'. I've met people that chat for ages before they meet and then are really disappointed, sod that, can't be bothered, and I'm sure the ones who don't want to meet are catfish, I've encountered many of those, the ones who never want to meet because their pic isn't of them, well trot on then, the second word is 'off.

I had that on the free one too though, gorgeous guy, very gorgeous, fabulous profile, said all the right things and when I showed a friend she googled the pic and it was a stock pic from an agency. I complained to them but that was it, never got any response. I've met men who've paid hundreds of pounds to join a site and the woman has disappeared as soon as they've paid up. A scam I'm absolutely sure and then there are the one or two who meet and it's all roses and weddings, if it's true, I'm sure some are, but not very many. Probably like weight loss, let's see if they're still together in a year, I sincerely doubt it.

I was getting loads of cock pics to my phone and Nadia would open them, probably not great for a ten year old but we're very open, since Alex left we've always walked around naked, I see nothing wrong with that, though Nadia will be disappointed if she thinks all men naked are as beautiful and adequate as her brother.

I met a guy on the free one who's profile attracted me because it said 'oops, spilt another drop' so I told him to meet me outside Tesco in Calne in fifteen minutes. He was rather surprised at the speed of the conversation, but if he passed the three second test we might be OK. I wasn't that attracted to him but he didn't look like an axe murderer and I didn't have anyone to go out with on Saturday nights when Alex had the children so Colin and his neighbour might be OK as pals. We got VERY drunk that first Saturday night, we got VERY drunk whenever we met. I roped in a woman from the playground whose husband had run off with a younger version and dragged her out with us too. We would go out on Friday and or Saturday nights and became friends. I think she fancied the neighbour in Calne, her ex was bald like the neighbour. The bald guy once remarked, "why did you leave Alex? I've never heard you say a bad word about him", thank goodness for that.

Colin was quite keen but I was into Harry and wasn't going to sleep with anyone else until I was sure he wasn't going to leave his partner. I tried my best to entice him but he wasn't having any of it. I introduced him to swingers clubs, as I'd confirmed he was a player. Madly I had this theory that Mum had given me, if I gave him a long leash he'll always sleep in my bed, of course he never did. The Black Eyed Pea's 'I gotta feelin' continues to remind me of him.

We would go to Birmingham for the evening which he loved. I never indulged but I like putting on 6" heels, a basque and stockings as much as anyone and I was no longer so fat and looked OK. It seemed to me that men with small dicks took their wives there to get a good portion. I hated that part of it, women lying on tables with legs akimbo and a line of men waiting to fuck them, horrible, absolutely horrible, and the husband having the control of which ones could fuck her and which ones couldn't. They might have the bat and ball but we have the playing field. It's always about control it seems to me.

I swear men will do anything for sex. You only have to watch anything David Attenborough is narrating to see how the male will pursue a female for sex, men are no different. I'm sure they thought I was a working girl at Leigh Delamere. I was there fairly often meeting men for coffee who I would never have the time of day for really, their face pics often looked OK. They always seemed OK until I met them, and even if I was a bit attracted they'd have some baggage that wasn't acceptable, like a wife. Completely ridiculous really but was I being the other woman that my father was always drawn to perhaps? Complete madness, but these things are SO subconscious I wonder if we don't even realise we're playing the same games.

One of the guys I met was from Bournemouth or thereabouts, he knew all about swingers clubs, was on his speed boat in Spain when he called one time. I only fucked him once but I was so skint and not interested but he just kept on and on. He was really attractive but I just wasn't attracted to him. I said, "no" loads of times but he wouldn't give up so I told him he could fulfill a fantasy of paying me for it, so he did, £300 for fifteen minutes, paid the electric, I was that skint I was grateful..

I did a largeish mortgage case and was due £2500, which was now a lot of money to me, after having very little since 2009. I'd lost weight, through exercise really, I was swimming a mile at lunchtimes and walking Luca for an hour daily. The only bit I couldn't move with exercise was my boobs, which had always been big so I contemplated, do I take the kids on holiday or have new boobs? They wanted £7500 in the UK for an uplift and implants, I'd need implants otherwise I'd lose the volume, or £2500 in Istanbul. On August 1st 2010 I flew to Istanbul and had a boob job. When I woke up after the op it felt like I had a breeze block on my chest the implants were SO heavy.

Just by chance I saw a picture in the local paper of Sam who'd just completed some sporting thing so I sent him a card with my number on it. He text and I went to his one very hot Sunday afternoon while Alex had the children. He had cricket on the TV, always sport, and after three hours of amiable chat we eventually hit the bedroom, I think he was just curious about my new boobs really, but he couldn't touch them, they were so swollen and tender, with loads of stitches. I'd cycled to his and as I came around the corner to home Alex pulled up in the car with the children, he wasn't happy, smelt a rat. He went home but at 2am he was standing at the foot of our bed which really made me jump. He'd read my texts and was furious but he had to understand we were over. He sent Sam vile texts so I never heard from him again for a very long time.

It was Mum and Dad's 50th wedding anniversary and they were having a party, to which I wasn't invited, but the children and Alex had to attend. I arranged to go with Harry to a Devon swingers club for one final liaison, he wasn't leaving her. I had to tell him about the guy with the speedboat because there was a chance he'd be there. He laughed and told me that one of the days he'd been to see me he'd had sex with his girlfriend when he woke up, he then went to Worcester and had sex with another, then Bristol with another and then me. He insisted he'd become so able because a previous girlfriend, of which there had been many, had demanded sex four or five times a day because she wanted to get pregnant and he was scared of her so just made himself able.

We went to the party and speedboat man was there, we said, "hi" and moved on. I was never interested in other men, I'm very much a one-man woman when I have the right man. I did snog a woman there, not for long, not really that interested.

We drove back to Worcester the next morning where I got the train home and that was it, end of Harry, I wish.

Colin picked me up. I did try and have a relationship with him, but it didn't last long. At a singles night in Swindon, they are dire affairs, I introduced him to a woman who he instantly fell head over heels in love with, albeit very temporarily, but it was too late, our time had passed when they finished.

After my boob job I wasn't wanted in our gang of four, felt like I'd been tossed out, no idea why really but I took the hint and left quietly. I was tired of random men and decided to not partake anymore so spent weekend evenings when the children were with Alex drinking more and more, watching horror films, crying about anything and writing suicide letters to Mum once I was off the planet. I would lose it and scream at the top of my voice, "I wish I were dead," when I fell out with the children, usually over Ben still going to Mum's every evening, it wasn't often, but it happened and I regret it, very, very much.

2011 was my 'annus horribilis'. I went to my doctor and told him I thought I was suffering with depression to which he replied, "Nici if you were depressed you wouldn't get out of bed in the morning," and I thought, "you try not getting out of bed with two children and a red setter?" and that was that. So I just upped alcohol, it's only a drug after all. I drank more and more, was up to two bottles a day, sometimes three at weekends, never in the daytime though, unless a weekend, then maybe, if we were out I'd succumb. Work was slack and money was tight, but I managed to find enough to drink, I'd rather drink than eat. I saw another doctor and did try anti-depressants once, I was so aware of this drug in my body, my heart rate and pulse increased, I just didn't like it so only took them for a couple of weeks

I gave up on dating sites, I'm not like other girls who have boyfriends so what was the point? So I went on sex dating sites, if I offered more

I just might have a chance surely? I found the biggest site I could and began my mission. I put a pic of my boobs and had 3000 hits overnight and 7000 in three days and hundreds of messages, literally hundreds which I duly trawled through to find nothing, nothing whatsoever, bar one who was slightly interesting.

He seemed ideal, was professional, lived fairly near, separated, divorcing, we got along like a house on fire and the torso pics seemed good. I didn't get to see his dick but he assured me it was plentiful. He was dark haired, 6'+, all was good, the conversation flowed beyond sex often as we knew some similar people. Then he said he'd been to a party and I'd been mentioned, now I was too curious so I called him and as he knew my name I needed to know his, so very reluctantly he revealed it, Nathan. I hadn't heard of him but could keep a secret and was satisfied with the outcome so all OK. Getting to meet him was proving difficult, he just wouldn't, however hard I tried to persuade him. Eventually I got fed up and deleted him, cross that he'd managed to string me along for so long, far beyond 'meet me or delete me'.

Some weeks later I was contacted about a job, the owner had the same surname as the sex site man so I asked how Nathan was. He laughed out loud and said, "well he was alright thirty years ago, he's dead". A few moments later the penny dropped. I realised who he was, the husband of someone I knew many, many years ago, someone we'd mentioned while we chatted. I'm not going there, so was glad I'd deleted him, but what was he doing on that sex site?

Of course I was looking for my prince in the wrong place. I would only fuck men I'd date but I wouldn't date, that's a lie, I only ever chose attached ones, that's why I didn't date. Single men terrified me, at least if they were attached I had a reason why they wouldn't date me, if they were single and wouldn't date me it might prove there was something wrong with me and I was fine, just fine...not.

I started having nightmares of the film 'Cathy Come Home'. I'd watched it with Mum years ago, old black and white with too many well spoken actors. The scene where she's at the railway station, and they come and forcibly remove her children and she's panicking and crying. I began thinking if, "I don't stop drinking that'll happen to me". The thought never lasted long because I bashed it out of my mind, but the nightmare kept recurring.

I met a man who was a teacher in the Black Horse one evening, he was handsome and intelligent but I acted like a whore as always. I tried not to, and just kissed him that night and the next time I met him but the time after that I took a bottle of pink and downed it for some courage. If I didn't give amazing sex why would he ever want to be with me, wasn't I still the fattest, ugliest, horriblest woman on this earth? I saw him a few times but he never wanted me as a girlfriend and I was still into Harry really.

There was also a Thierry Henry/Lewis Hamilton lookalike who was gorgeous, very gorgeous, in a relationship with an older woman but his cock was a bit big, couldn't sit on it without lifting an inch or so up, beautiful though and had a brain, a plus I find. He split with his partner later and asked me out, I couldn't do that, why would he ever want to do that, why would he want to out with me? Most odd.

There was a bouncer in Bristol too, really fit and good looking, but that accent, not my cup of tea, passed the three second test in Castle Combe one afternoon so I drove to his later. He had a bag of party tricks, powders and potions, heavens only knows what it was, though I've since learned probably GHD, or is that hair straightners? Anyway, this stuff made for AMAZING amorous sex and wore off in an hour, he gave me a small bottle of it. Next time I saw Lewis we tried it, but didn't measure it in a syringe and it knocked us both out for hours.

I became quite friendly with Jordan the younger handsome client whose fiancé had left him. He was a bit 'Philip Schofield' an expression I used when I couldn't figure out if a man was gay or not. We decided to go and see a play in Bath together. He was twenty or more years younger than me but so pretty and I liked his company so why not, he wasn't attracted to me, it was just an excuse to get dressed up and go out and get drunk, he liked a drink too. He told me his fiancé left because she didn't like the fact that he would go to London and come home with hundreds of pounds which he insisted wealthy women gave him just to sit at a bar with them. Seemed likely to me, I wasn't going to pay but I liked going out with him and we sometimes ended up snogging in a doorway until one day I dragged him to the park and stuck my hand down his trousers, nope, not going there, wouldn't fit.

One evening we were so drunk I left the car unlocked in a car park and when we returned later it wasn't there (I drank and drove continuously) so we got a cab back to his. We rolled into bed and snogged but he wouldn't let me anywhere near his dick so I just laid back and enjoyed it, thank you very much. I reported my car stolen the next day. A few days later my cousin text and told me my car was in a car park on the other side of town. Kids were in the first car park when we'd arrived, they must've realised I hadn't locked it and nicked it, but the petrol light was flashing so they'd dumped it in the nearest car park they could. It had loads of tickets on it and I had a real battle with the council to cancel them.

Jordan was very popular with a few very good looking women, which I was not and one night when we were out I was chatting to someone I knew and realised her friend was waiting for him to return from Bath, where we'd been for the evening. I blew a text fuse at him the next day for using me to fill time while he waited for her, I was SO angry, how dare he. Why didn't he just come out and be honest like all gay men who want kids, find an unattractive, plain women who'd be glad to have such a handsome husband, get the kids and have a real life behind her back, like the rest of them. We've not spoken since but I did hear that he moved in with a man sometime later.

Our divorce came through in 2011, or was it 2012, it didn't matter, no one knew and there was nothing to split. There was no money and the children had no idea anything was going on, or so I thought. Then recently I heard Ben tell a friend of his that us parting was the worst thing that had ever happened in his whole life, I had no idea. I do wonder if it's why he's bald. I think stress manifests itself in different ways in every single one of us. Grandma has a picture of the hundreds of men who were working at Westinghouse, an engineering firm, in Chippenham around 1910, before the First World War, the children's Great, Great Grandfather is on it. Not one man is bald, not one, or obese.

I spent many evenings thinking about drinking the whole bottle of stuff the Bristolian guy had given me, it was in my bedside table drawer, I looked at it often. All I had to do was swig it down and I'd be off this planet, forever, that was all I had to swig it quickly, it was vile stuff.

WHAT PROBLEM

We'd moved around the corner on the same street and the children were having all their friends back regularly while I was drunk in bed in the evenings. Ben would have fifteen to twenty friends over on a Friday and Saturday night and I didn't see anything wrong with it. They'd all smoke in the garage, sometimes weed I think but at least they were safe and together.

With little to do I decided to attempt the family tree as Dad had always frowned when I mentioned it and uttered, "you don't want to do that," so I was curious. I discovered Nan was a gypsy, and that was why when mentioned by other aunts they would say, "she did well, considerin'". In that moment I forgave Dad for all his affairs, I concluded that he must have been bullied and ridiculed in the school playground and realising his trump card was his looks he used them to his best advantage. A way of getting back at society perhaps for the shame he felt, his 'fuck you' button, literally.

In 2012 I got a job, at last, as mortgage broking had completely gone for me. The job was part-time as a barmaid in a pub at Sutton Benger, I knew the landlord and his family. It wasn't really a good idea because I drank while I was there and would drive home very drunk often but it got me out of the house rather than sitting at home drinking alone. It only lasted a few months as the pub got taken over by new people in the summer and I didn't like the owner that ran it so I left.

I happened to see 'Bed Knobs and Broomsticks' at Christmas and when the old lady on the steps of St Pauls appeared I thought, "if I don't stop drinking that's going to be me," of course the modern version of that is the old lady in Central Park in 'Home Alone' both could resemble me in a few years if I kept my drinking up.

We went camping with Luca in Newquay and I had a single gas ring explode while I was crouched over it frying something, the canister was in upside down apparently, it worked though. I hadn't had a drink, it was 4pm, I was about to but hadn't. The fire burnt all the skin on my face and took my hair and I had third degree burns on my fingers. An ambulance was called and we all went to Plymouth in an ambulance and I got very high on the gas and air, not Luca though, some kind people kept him. The paramedic completed a form on the way, he asked how much I drank and I said, "a couple". He replied, "a couple of glasses a week," to which I laughed, the gas was working well, "no, a couple of bottles a day," I said, his eyes widened and the children said, "she doesn't get drunk". Mum and Dad drove down to take us all home, Mum drove my car back, we hadn't spoken in years, the children saw them most weeks but not me, it was a little tense.

A week or two afterwards Nadia said, "mummy all your wrinkles have gone", not the best way to have a chemical peel I suppose but there was a benefit. Soon after that Social Services came knocking, they always do apparently if children are involved. The social worker interviewed them without me there and all was fine but she gave me a leaflet from an alcohol and drugs charity on New Road and said perhaps I should consider getting help with my alcohol problem. What problem?

Alex had been internet dating, at last, and met Julie who he brought to the pub with the children to meet me, she was nice and had children too, I was so glad he'd found someone at last. On the next Mothers' Day I bought a card for the children to give to her and they wrote 'to our second mum', I needed her onside and thought this might pay dividends.

A few weeks later Nadia and Ben were at Mum and Dad's for Sunday lunch, which they sometimes did when I wasn't around. Alex called me and asked me to collect Nadia from his and then told me what had happened, Mum had slapped Nadia around the face. I wasn't speaking to them so I went to the police station to ask them to have a word with Mum and tell her that's not acceptable. They said they could put Mum in a cell for the night, I wished, but I did refrain. Next thing Social Services are back with, "you should seek help with your drinking," so I thought, "I'll show them, I'll show them I'm not an alcoholic", and made an appointment at the charity on New Road.

In August 2012 I walked into New Highway, the charity, for this appointment, sat down with a lady, looked at her, took a deep breath and burst into tears. I spent the whole hour sobbing, absolutely sobbing. Our session finished and there was an auricular acupuncture session starting so I stayed for it. I met people who got me, who understood, other drug and alcohol users. I had two more appointments with the lady and during the next year they put me on courses including an NLP course and an acupuncture one. I loved it all, I loved the people, being with them and having something to do but I didn't get very sober. They advised me not to drink before 6pm and restrict it to one bottle a day. Well that was OK, for the first week, and then I was back up to two and three bottles but at least I got out a bit and did stuff with them.

While I was on one of the courses I insisted I had a food problem, not an alcohol problem but slowly I began to wonder, when I drank I always drank to get off the planet so maybe. De-nial, is not just a river in Egypt.

They'd taught me to do acupuncture and one day I went to do a session in Chippenham and there were two men waiting for the session in the car park. I looked at this man and thought, "maybe I should have a fat man, everyone else seems to be OK with a fat man", he looked like the Forever Friends Bear to me and when we were introduced he said he went to AA so that Monday night, with nothing better to do, I went to AA.

I went with the guy who I did acupuncture with, he was kind and very happy to take me along. The Bear was there, with his friend, and there were a lot of other people there too. I just kept my head down and listened, I was used to the format, I'd been before to OA back in 1990. The woman that shared talked about her drinking being like a revolving door. She said she just kept going round and round 360 degrees, and wanting to get off at 180 degrees for something to change, I could identify with that.

I didn't drink in that week. I thought, "if I can get it down to a bottle on Friday, Saturday and Sunday that'd be really good". And so I did, Friday came and I had one bottle and the same on Saturday and Sunday. I went to the meeting on Monday and when people asked how my week had been I told them it'd been good, controlling my drinking like this worked, I had this sussed. The following week it was the bank holiday so I had one on Thursday, after all it was a holiday, then it was two on Friday night, three on Saturday night and when I got to the fourth on Sunday I knew they were right, I was wrong, IT controlled me, I couldn't control IT. And that was my last alcoholic drink, I remember pouring half a bottle of £7 white wine down the sink thinking, "this **HAS** to stop".

I went to the meeting the next night and listened again, I chatted with the Bear, he'd been sober eight months or so. We became friendly and I started to go to more meetings, most evenings and daytimes. I liked the people and it was keeping me sober. People were kind, they'd come up and tell you to keep coming back, it'll work if you work it. I spoke (shared) for the first time one Saturday morning at a really busy meeting where they left the last ten minutes for newcomers and shy sharers. I said I'd been sober two weeks and this record I'd had all my life, "everybody hates you, it's all your fault, you're thick, you're fat, you're ugly," had gone quiet, it was still there, but way, way back and I could barely hear it and I thanked them for their love and support.

After the meeting a man I'd met at the Monday meeting came over and introduced me to a very tall man who shook my hand and said, "I really liked what you said, keep coming back," I thanked him and we chatted briefly, everyone was so kind. I began to wish I'd had the courage to go to AA rather than OA back in 1990.

The Bear had three dogs and had just got a job. His wife had left him with their two boys who were similar ages to Ben and Nadia. I volunteered my dog walking services and would go to his and walk Luca with his three Labradors, I enjoyed it, I had little other work. He offered to pick me up to take me to meetings with his friend which made me happy. I got a sponsor who would help me work the steps and was there if I wobbled, she was years and years sober and just lovely.

The Bear turned up to collect me one day without his sidekick and on the way to the meeting asked me if I'd go out with him, I was elated. Nobody had ever asked me that before, ever, and I SO wanted him. I could fix him, I could make it all better for him, I understood him and his problems, it was all going to be rosy, I was instantly up the aisle in my head. We walked Luca and he kissed me, his mouth completely covered mine, I didn't like it and later told him as diplomatically as possible. Please could he kiss me like this and gave a demonstration. He never kissed me again. When he came to mine I'd sit on his lap, like a child wanting a cuddle from their father and of course that was what I was doing because I never had been cuddled by my father that I could recall. Within a week we went for coffee and he said, "when are you going to make up with your Mum and Dad? You'll have to, I need to ask him if I can marry you," it made me SO happy, I was over the moon. That night his children were away and so I stayed over. Sober sex, now that was a completely new experience, for both of us, he wasn't disappointed. I swung from chandeliers as usual and pulled every trick I could think of in my book. We barely slept a wink.

From then on Nadia and I would spend the whole weekend at his, the children got on, though Ben always stayed home as his friends would come over. Everything seemed wonderful but he would question me if I was five minutes late, and I was often a lot later with stuff to do, like a home and children to organise. Some people in AA were keeping a keen eye on proceedings, it's frowned on to get into a relationship in early recovery because they're so difficult emotionally and often the first thing to make us pick up a drink again, but we weren't like that were we? It's called thirteenth stepping. An old sage said to me, "Nici, don't make him your higher power," which I laughed off, "of course I wouldn't make him my hp, would I?" Of course I did. When he was up I was up, when he was down he wouldn't call and it was like Chinese torture. I would go crazy worrying he didn't want me or like me anymore. He was very controlling, maybe I was too, hence clashing often, reeling me in and in and in and then pushing me away when I got too close. He had to be in control and didn't really want me close at all. I don't think he can stand anyone being close, which might be why we found each other, to reveal the problem as it was a problem I'd always had. He bought expensive tickets for a New Year's Eve Ball with his old friends and in the weeks leading up to it we were on and off like a tart's knickers. We were going, then we weren't, we were, then we weren't. Nadia got fed up of messaging her friends that their party at his with his boys was on then off, on then off.

He bought me a very expensive cream beaded long gown for this New Year's Eve bash. I showed Nadia and she didn't like it, I was unsure, it reminded me of a wedding dress. So I took it back and bought a Lipsy short purple sparkly backless body con dress which looked fabulous, even if I do say so myself, especially with 6" heels. I'd lost weight no longer drinking alcohol.

Christmas came and he said his son wanted, "a Nici free Christmas," and he didn't do presents, so all the romanticism was null and void. Nadia and I went to his on Boxing Day but he was so foul we left after an hour or two, much to his surprise. He plays that card with his current girlfriend too, so cruel.

The ball came and went, taking very drunk people home as you're the only ones sober isn't great fun, it was something of nothing really, did love the disco though, always love a disco, with the right music.

We continued. I got a job with a mortgage company but after doing their course they didn't want me, telling the head of financial services his presentation was rubbish didn't go down too well, how was I to know who he was? The Bear didn't last in his sales job either but I reassured him it was meant to be and something else would come along that was more his cup of tea, he liked my positivity. He then shaved his head, an act of defiance really, it wasn't a good look. We went to a lunchtime meeting one day and I heard this well-spoken man and looked out the corner of my eye and thought to myself, "I'm going out with him next". I had no clue who he was.

At coffee with some friends after a meeting we were talking about men and one of them told me I needed to read, 'Women who love too much' by Robin Norwood. I read it in a day, it was a mirror.

At the next meeting I sat next to a woman who showed me a £600 handbag she was going to buy herself for her six months sober present and I thought to myself "I'm six months sober tomorrow, I know what I'm going to do, I'm getting rid of him," and I did. He wasn't happy and called and called. Then he text and I replied, daily, which I loved, I wanted him to chase me and he did, for a while, then I didn't reply and he turned up at my door. I told him to read the book, we were both love addicts, but he wasn't interested, he knows it all. He already had another girlfriend, the woman he dated twenty-five years ago, before his wife. He had mentioned that he'd popped in for coffee while visiting his Mum and I thought nothing of it, I'd asked if that was all and he said, "yes". I'm not a liar and I don't expect other people to be, it can be a mistake. There are no mistakes, there are only lessons.

A new lady shared at a meeting that when she'd read the steps she thought to herself 'they've missed one, where's the one where they make amends to me for what they've done to me'. Everybody laughed, because we can't change others, we can only change ourselves so we have to take responsibility for our part in it, for the harm we caused. But in the back of my mind I agreed with her, I will never believe I would have been a food and love addict if I'd felt loved as a child.

LETTING GO

It was tortuous, the pain of losing love (or was it the fantasy) was immense and so I returned to food and started bingeing and purging. Not for long though, a month or so, but I didn't drink alcohol. I just kept going to meetings, as many as I could, a lot of them, and managed to get through it.

I asked Ben why he wasn't fond of the Bear and he said, "because he took you away from me," and my heart sank. He was right of course, I was completely consumed in my love addiction because it fixed me, it felt SO nice when it was good but the reality was that it wasn't good that often in the end, it was tortuous. The reality didn't match the fantasy.

A lot of Ben's friends have stepfathers, and now that they're young men they're being tossed out of the nest by the mother's new partner. Two lions don't last in one den. Why do we put our happiness over our children's? I suppose the children are going to leave one day, or are they? This is a very different world. I doubt if a careers advisor tells girls they're going to be married with children at nineteen anymore, I certainly hope that isn't what they tell them.

I did my step four with my sponsor, that 'searching and fearless moral inventory'. I wrote my life story, thought Ruth Jones might take it and make it into a film but no, I had to burn it, in my sacred spot, on my Nan's grave, so I did.

In retaliation I thought it might be a good idea to contact Harry, on the off chance that he just might be single, how ridiculous was that. He was now married to another woman who had said, "marry me or leave," and he didn't fancy moving back in with his Dad so he married her. We agreed to meet on an afternoon at a service station with rooms, very glamorous and romantic, and that became a regularish monthly thing. He did confess that when we first met he had twenty of us on the go. I asked him one day, curled up warm and safe after another marathon of unrivalled passion, what his mother was like and he said he never knew what he'd get when he came in from school, whether she'd be happy and with it, or suicidal, she suffered with mental illness problems and had died a few years back. His father was still alive though and living in his old house. It made me think of what Ben must think about me.

I always said, "hi" to everyone I could at a meeting, but especially people I didn't recognise, they could be visiting or new so the most important person in the room. This day there was a beautiful 6'+ red-haired man alone in the corner so I went over, said "hi", introduced myself and asked if he was visiting. "No, I came out of rehab yesterday," so the conversation and enthusiasm flowed and I introduced him to another guy of a similar age. I sat down next to my friend and said, "oh my god, I hope he's married". Fortunately he was, with two children. I never understood why I was so attracted to red haired men and then my children bought me a DNA testing kit which revealed I was 30% Scandinavian, so I assume that's it. It also said I was 30% English and 30% Irish, Scottish and Welsh, 9% Eastern European, Romania? Gypsies? and 1% tip of India, which is where gypsies come from apparently. It was from Heritage, the US version of Ancestry I think so maybe the emphasis is different.

I've worked out I'm attracted to men who make me feel small, so long as they're taller, or broader, or preferably both I'm attracted, hair colour doesn't make any difference whatsoever, providing they have some, and their own teeth and are lively, physically fit, interesting and solvent and within 10 years of me, older or younger, but I'm finding the older ones can't usually keep up, on a dog walk.

I got to step nine where we try to make amends to those we have harmed and decided to write notes to those I thought had been adversely affected by my behaviour. With hindsight I had this bit wrong because the word *sorry* isn't mentioned but I used it a lot and hand delivered them, bar Simon's that I gave to his sister to send to him as I had no idea where he was now living.

I delivered one of these notes, knocked on the door, hoping every time in all honesty that no one was in. A lady opened the door, she looked like the old lady in 'Home Alone' or 'Bed Knobs and Broomsticks'. I didn't know who it was but handed the note over and asked if she'd give it to the person in question, and it was her, I couldn't believe it, that would've been me in a few years' time.

I wrote a nine-page letter to Mum and Dad at the same time, we'd not spoken in years, asking "why did everybody hate me, why was it all my fault?" amongst many other things. I showed it to my sponsor, she said, "are you going to send it?" "Yes" I said. "Well I suggest you take out that, that, this, that, that, that, that". I ended up with a page of 'I love you, thank you very much'.

On my years anniversary of being sober I knocked on their door, hoping no one was in but Mum was. She was surprised to see me. I gave her the letter and she beckoned me inside. She read the letter and cried and said, "that's SO lovely, I always knew it was your fault".

I went home and told Nadia what I'd done, she told me to tell Ben. Ben had maintained contact with Mum and Dad, he was there most evenings. They sat on the sofa next to me and with my head bowed low in shame I told them I'd given Nanny a letter and said "sorry for anything I might have said or done that harmed or offended you". As I looked up they were both crying, it was only at that moment I realised how much my drinking had affected them. We cried together and hugged, there is SO much love in our home between these four walls.

The phone went, it was Nanny, did we want to go out for dinner with her and Grampy, it was their wedding anniversary after all. We went to The Fox and the children got someone to take a photograph of us all. Later they put the photo on Facebook as I did. I wrote, "The power of nine, thank you all". Nadia and Ben put the same photo up with, "Mum's been sober a year today and made up with Nan and Gramp", never very anonymous.

Between Christmas and New Year I arranged to meet with some NA (Narcotics Anonymous) people for dinner. There were six of us, I knew all of them bar one and he turned out to be the well-spoken guy that I heard that day months before when I'd thought to myself, "I'm going to go out with him next," and he lived on my side of Bath. He wrote his number on a piece of paper and said, "call me, come over for a dog walk, I live in private woods", seemed like a good idea so I messaged him a few weeks later and took Luca over for a walk.

We got on well, he was the right age, tall enough, seemed fairly fit and I liked his look albeit a bit casual but it was OK. We became friends and he then asked me to have a relationship with him, which was flattering but I was unsure. He lived half his time on the other side of the world with a partner and her two children, one of which is his, that can't be a good idea. He asked me to stay one evening when we got back to his, we had kissed once, but I wanted so much more so I declined telling him I didn't want to mess this up so I wouldn't stay, we have all the time in the world for this after all. The next day I was consumed with him, desperately wanting to sleep with him, it seems that when I do the right thing and decline my head then panics and says, "NO, you need it NOW". The next night we'd arranged to go to a party so I decided I was going to stay after his invitation the previous evening. After we got back to his and drank tea I mentioned that I would like to stay and he said, "no, it's not a good idea," I was gutted. I wanted him to say he'd leave her and I'd move over there so he could be near his daughter but that wasn't happening so in frustration I went back to the sex site, pushing my 'fuck it' button again.

Although life had become a lot better in many respects, no longer drinking, what it took longer to realise is that I'm self-medicating and if I put one thing down I pick up something else to do the job. It's never about what I do, it's always about why I do it, it's solving that little puzzle that's key.

There were some statistics that came out around this time. When we go to A&E they ask us how much we drink and smoke. The first time I went to A&E in sobriety when she asked that I cried. We're 12 MILLION bottles short A WEEK!! The difference between what we tell the NHS we drink and what is sold in the supermarkets was 12 MILLION BOTTLES A WEEK. And it's not the kids that are drinking it, it's the forty +'s, we're the ones going to A&E falling down, in fact it's worse in the generation before me, the sixty +'s.

So I was back on the sex site and wasn't messing around this time, I searched men within five miles and found three or four instantly. One I dismissed straight away. Another insisted I call him, so I did, nervously, though why I don't know, we seemed to click, I liked his pics and he mine so I told him I was meeting this other one and would get back to him. He was in a relationship with two children but this was just some NSA. Another coffee at Leigh Delamere with the third one and I wasn't the least bit interested so I arranged to meet the phone call for the three second test.

We met on a cold wet afternoon. He got out of his car and my jaw dropped instantly, he was perfect, just what I'd always wanted. Bearded, 6'+, fit, intelligent, articulate, professional, perfect and I'd already seen him naked in pics so I knew all that. He wanted to get in the car there and then but I refused, he kissed me and I melted, perfect, just perfect.

We chatted a lot online over the following days and arranged to meet after a week or so but I couldn't do it and cancelled. He was too much my cup of tea, just exactly what I'd always wanted in a partner so I told him this and he said he was flattered and understood, but this was definitely NSA so if I wanted more it wasn't happening.

After declining, as usual, my head became completely consumed with him and a week or two later he came to my house and it was heaven, just heaven. Cocks are rather like shoes, I like them to fit, his was the most perfect fit ever. We lay on the bed after passionate sex and talked and I told him a part of my story about alcoholism and food addiction, I'm always too damn open and honest. Then I mentioned that this could be an addiction, he was curious, so I explained that if it's just me, him and his partner it's probably OK, had to make me OK obviously. But my other friend, for instance, has many, many women and he's addicted to it, he doesn't realise it, he just thinks he likes variety in sex but he's addicted to it and the truth is he probably doesn't even like women. He fucks so many women because he actually doesn't like them, because his mother was never there for him, because she was ill. He never knew if she'd be well or ill when he got in from school so fucking loads of women is his way of saying 'fuck you' to women, of course Harry completely disagreed and said I was, "talking jack-shit," but that's the truth of it from a psychological viewpoint.

I told Perfect about SLAA and SAA (Sex and Love Addicts Anonymous and Sex Addicts Anonymous) same stuff as AA, different people often, there are loads of different fellowships, loads, yet in truth the problem is the same. Isolation, feeling we don't belong, not being good enough and we find or learn something, anything, that makes us feel better and use it and then IT becomes the problem when it never is, it's never about what we do, it's always about why we do it.

We chatted a lot, morning noon and night over the next couple of months and met intermittently. I went to his house while his partner was away. It was all great but once he wanted anal and I've never liked that but was so in to him I obliged, why do they like that? Is it because it's so tight? flipping hurts, not pleasurable at all, I know there's a very fine line between pain and pleasure but why, if someone say it hurts, why would you want to continue doing it? Sadistic. He wants to hurt women, that's why. We met in lay bys, at his, at mine, all very exciting, naughty and exhilarating but as I drew closer he pulled away.

THE PREDATOR

That same Christmas I was devastated that he hadn't called, I was desperate for his attention. Then a friend asked me to share at a meeting so I agreed to lighten this load of heartache, thought it might help. It was a quiet lunchtime meeting and I told my story saying I came here because I fancied a Bear in a car park and that I was given the record of 'you're thick, fat, ugly, unlovable etc'. The man who'd had himself introduced to me and had been so kind every time I'd seen him, he was kind to everyone, shared back, "Nici, please believe me when I tell you there isn't a man in this room who doesn't wish he was that Bear", my heart pounded, we always say we have to own our stuff, so he was saying that to me, I was quite overcome, the love addict in me was rife, what a shame he was many years happily married. He went on to say perhaps I should consider another fellowship, I was puzzled but later realised he was talking about SLAA and SAA.

When I mentioned what he'd said to a friend who knew him she said, "but you look a bit like his first wife", I'd never thought of that. I respected him and his recovery though, he didn't do alcohol, drugs, caffeine or sugar that I was aware, walking a path I wanted to follow.

I did try SLAA a month or two later and they made me block him immediately saying he was predatory. I didn't agree, he was just kind, ridiculous really, he was very happily married. The Predator and I had a mutual friend who was struggling and so he had text me a few times and called, reluctantly I blocked him, it felt very rude, he was only being supportive. I was taking a very small meeting at that time and he turned up at the next meeting, much to my surprise. My heart pounded and I was trembling inside, but this too shall pass, and it did. So I stopped taking the meeting and going anywhere he might be which wasn't that difficult really, it just kept me safe, I don't like that pounding heart feeling anymore. It's like being at the top of a rollercoaster, exhilarating, exciting, addictive and there's only one way out and it's down, into misery, pain, rejection, suffering. I heard Lulu's '*Boom-bang-a-bang*' on Paul Gambaccini and it reminded me of my pounding heart and him, still does.

I didn't particularly think SLAA helped me so looked elsewhere for help and even started a CODA meeting, Co-dependents Anonymous, where you're addicted to fixing everyone around you avoiding your own stuff, my mother would be a prime candidate for that one, always got her nose in other people's business when the problem is her.

In the end I went to ACOA, Adult Child of Alcoholics and Dysfunctional families, I got top marks to enter that one. It helped a lot, just finding people who have had a similar experience and don't tell you it's all your fault, you're the crazy one, you're the problem, people who care and love you back to a healthier happier you.

I realised I was probably going through the menopause after reading that we're very fertile as we approach it which is no doubt also why I'd fallen pregnant at forty-five or so. It also explained why I'd forced sex on Alex six or seven times one night while we camped at Woolacombe then with the children too. So I thought HRT might help and got some from my doctor. Oh, my flipping god! My libido went through the roof, I was watching porn two and three times a day and using my bullet, the batteries were being changed weekly! And I felt high, couldn't bear it, there must an anti-depressant in there too. I knew I'd have trouble getting off of them so stopped them after a few weeks.

I was bored so I got back on the free dating site determined to do it properly this time, dating and all that. I found this man whose name was familiar, Brad, it rang bells with me. We arranged to meet in the Angel for coffee. He wasn't pretty but he was such fun, we chatted for ages, had loads in common, knew similar people and he asked me to go for dinner on Saturday night in Bath so I agreed. On the journey, I told him I didn't drink and why and revealed all, as usual, which he respected. Little did I realise quite how familiar his name was, he was world famous in Bath, we couldn't walk twenty yards without someone wanting to shake his hand, people just came up to him in the restaurant and the bars. A very popular man indeed and lovely too.

The next day he asked to meet me for coffee so we met at Allington Farm Shop, and again, people were coming up and saying hi, which was fine. When the coffee arrived and it was quieter he leaned over the table, took my hand and said there was something he wanted to tell me, something he'd never told anyone before, ever. He'd told me about a lot of girlfriends, a lot, and that he could fuck his ex for hours but never come. He then told me that as a young boy there was a man down the road who raped him, and he suspected his brother. This man was ten years or more, older than him but regularly did this to him, it made him so angry and he felt so powerless as a small child that he vowed to become big and strong so it could never happen again. He was certainly big and strong, always had been. He had tears in his eyes as he told me, as did I. I just held his hands, and listened as the story unfolded, and I loved him, with my eyes I loved him, that's all I could do. I couldn't go back and undo what had been done but I could love him, listen and be there now.

He worked some evenings and would call to meet me afterwards which was OK but not ideal. We met in a pub and afterwards he asked me to go for a drive so I left my car and got in his. We drove to a spot he knew, kissed, a bit of groping ensued with boobs and cock out. He got out of the car, walked around to my side, opened my door and had sex with me from behind, not exactly what I'd wanted to happen, but he didn't come. I kind of like the mess oddly, perhaps I feel like I've done what I meant to, like the cream on the cake hilariously, though it was never really hilarious.

A week went by and I didn't hear from him, then another, I was gutted, I really liked him, even if he wasn't pretty, he was kind and caring and warm. Eventually I text him and he replied 'I don't think we'll ever be partners Nic, but we can be friends'. I burst into tears, I'd done it again, fucked too soon and he was gone, I was absolutely gutted and deleted him vowing never to get on the free one or a dating site again, and I haven't, been on a dating app, just a sex one, when will I learn!

I found some photos of Dad with his beard aged fortyish and realised that was why I'd looked at Perfect and fallen for him, he looked just like my Dad when he had a beard. Harry and Pete also looked a bit like Dad in some strange way and I wondered if The Predator had done something similar with me as I looked a little like his mother, as did his first wife my friend had once commented. And Colin had fallen hook line and sinker for the woman at the singles night and when I met his mother she was her double. They, whoever 'they' are, say we're attracted to those who look like our siblings or parents and it does seem to be true, for me anyway.

I let the kids have parties sometimes, only four of them over three years, after prom, at the end of term, for a birthday and New Year's Eve. Quite a lot would turn up, about one hundred and thirty each time but they were always well behaved and no trouble. I made them pay £2 each after the first one because it cost that for the carpet cleaner and speakers, and usually a little bit of damage, a window or cheap table got broken. I always warned the neighbours, assuring them it'd all be over by eleven or twelve at the latest, bar the New Year's Eve one which went on until 1am. A police car turned up at the first one so I went and greeted him and he was fine knowing there was a sober adult in charge. The other two parties passed with no problems, I called the police myself to get rid of unwanted guests at them.

Then one day I got home and there were loads of police cars about. Some of Nadia's friend had jumped our fence and broken in to a derelict cricket pavilion behind us. Some nosey parker had called the police and they were marching these fourteen year old children off like they were thugs, in hand cuffs with arms behind their backs, I thought their actions very over the top and so filmed it on my phone. One of the officers got very angry being filmed and attacked me to take my phone, then another did the same. Eventually they forcibly took my phone from me then asked me for my phone number, idiots.

I'd already contacted one of the parents concerned and they went to the police station to retrieve their child and the rest followed.

I lodged a complaint with the Police Complaints Authority and was fobbed off, as usual, they never do anything wrong do they?

The next time the kids had a party Wiltshire Police's Sergeant Sweeney was pointing his finger in my face shouting, "I'm going to get you evicted," and he did.

HOMELESS

We moved to homeless accommodation in Trowbridge in January 2016 thinking the council would house us within a few weeks but they didn't. It was a tough time, really tough, I started bingeing and purging again and got back on the sex site and met random men again, it was absolutely horrible. Perfect found me on the site and put a verification up, I was rather surprised 'this woman is fit and fabulous' but he still didn't want to see me. I just wanted to be loved, as usual, and never ever was. I was looking for a partner, giving sex to get love and of course I never ever did, get love. Women use sex to get love, men use love to get sex, it's rather like women are from venus, men are from mars, and never shall the twain meet, seems true enough to me.

I met a few men, usually in car parks. Sometimes I'd get in the car endure a chat and say "no", sometimes I didn't even bother with the five-minute chat, just turned up, took one look at them and said "no". I never met anyone I was interested in, bar Harry and Perfect. I told one guy, "I only fuck men I'd date but I don't date", how crazy is that, what I was saying was, "I only fuck men I'd marry but they never want me". I wonder why not? I did see a couple for one off sex around that time, I think four of them in a few weeks, or was it two weeks? Providing the equipment looked like the right size, so when I sat on it, it felt like it touched my belly button, I do love that feeling. Didn't particularly like any of them was just desperate to be wanted, kissed, hugged, loved and that was the last time I had sex, sort of.

I tried going a bit up market with my sex sites, and I was on one that a friend had mentioned. I met some nice people online and arranged to go to one of their parties, a masquerade ball, in Mayfair. It was OK, men were in black tie, we all wore masks until 11pm but my experience is that women do not want to share their man, unless they want rid of him. And women in relationships do not want single women around. The couples I met were at this party because the men wanted to be there, not the women. Secure women don't mind sharing their man it seems, but those not married or insecure, they don't want to share their man, which is fine and understandable but why put up with going? Why do we go that far to try and keep a man? The women can approach men at these parties but the men can't approach women, which is good because men will do anything for sex. There was a beautiful man there, with a beard, so as he walked past I touched his hand and asked if he were alone, he wasn't, but smiled and carried on. A few minutes later I was with the people I'd met attempting sex with the male of one of the couples but he couldn't get it up a second time and the man I'd approached watched on with his very beautiful partner. Later I realised that's how it works, if I'd have beckoned him then he'd have obliged but I missed my chance, probably just as well. I didn't stay long, an hour or two most, and drove home.

Oddly we grew to love living in that one bedroom flat, brought us really close together, sleeping in one room, quite loved it in the end, in fact if I had the choice I'd live like that permanently, though not there.

It's crazy really. We all aspire to live in big houses as far away from others as possible to show how successful we are and yet there are villages high in the hills in Italy or Greece that I recall, where they found the longest living, healthiest and happiest people. They live in small terraced houses, almost on top of each other. They meet every day in the piazza and talk. The researchers thought it was the healthy Mediterranean diet that kept them living so long, but it wasn't. Then they thought it must be the fresh air, but it wasn't that either. What they discovered, much to their surprise was that it was eye to eye contact that kept these people happy and healthy, not being alone and away from each other in massive houses. Eye to eye contact is SO important, ask Edwin Starr. Any place where we meet with people is good for us, it's isolation that isn't good for us and I wonder if screens are isolation? That's also why the fellowships work I'm sure, eye to eye contact, just love and support really.

We were evicted from the homeless place in September after an investigation in to whether or not we'd made ourselves 'intentionally homeless' and they concluded that we had which was rubbish, I'd let my children have parties, there was clearing up to do and we did it. This was about Sergeant Sweeney wanting to punish me for complaining about the police and filming them being bullies to fourteen-year-old children.

Everybody in NA had told me they wouldn't separate a mother and fifteen year old daughter, but they did, they didn't give a damn so Nadia and Ben went to live with Mum and Dad as they were still both at school in Chippenham. Mum didn't want me living there, we rarely spoke, and I figured that if I lived in a tent that would force the council to house me, it didn't.

Dad had the field at Tiddleywink, the one his Grandfather had to keep horses he traded at the market, he'd bought it from his brothers. My cousin and I put up his large tent in the field and I lived there throughout October. I quite liked it actually, I'd swim and shower at the leisure centre and I had my queen size bed in it and being alone, I loved it. It was sunny and quite lovely but Nadia didn't cope well. Surprised me really, I thought all they did was ignore me, tell me I'm bi-polar and moan about not being a good cook and yet when I'm not there they don't cope very well at all it seems. Perhaps they do love me really and miss my love for them when I'm not around, perhaps my kissing them and telling them I love them every day matters, not that I didn't do that while living in the tent but perhaps it is the eye to eye contact that really matters.

I was getting a lot of hot flushes while I lived there though, stress of the situation I suppose, I was eating a lot of crap too, sugar and flour again, no doubt that's what caused the hot flushes, sugar always does and hot food or drinks I found do it too. I just couldn't see how I was ever going to get out of it, how I was ever going to find a house to rent. I contacted Perfect, just for some respite, wanted to see him just to make myself feel a bit better. I didn't get to ask him to meet me, he was reading the SLAA handbook. He'd acknowledged he had a sex addiction problem, was in therapy and his therapist confirmed what I'd told him, that his relationship with his mother hadn't been good and so his sex addiction was a way of getting back at women, he wanted to hurt them, which explained a lot, didn't want it to be true really, but it is. He called me a week or so later and I put him in touch with a man I knew in Bath who was in SAA, I knew that'd be the last time I heard from him, you can't contact anyone you acted out with once you're in SAA or SLAA.

I was emailing every three-bedroom house for up to £750pm that came on the market to rent, desperately trying to find one that would accept an ex bankrupt on housing benefit but I rarely got a reply. Then one day the phone went and it was the agents for a cottage I'd applied for. They called to say that the landlord had said that the house wasn't quite big enough for three adults so I thanked her for being so kind to have called, it was just nice to get a response at all. The next day the same number called and I said, "you called yesterday, I know we can't have it," to which she said, "no, the landlord knows you and said you can have it, providing everything is OK with references". I was over the moon. It was, is, my dream home a three-bed terraced cottage, just outside of a village. The landlord's agent was an old mortgage client of mine, what a relief, we had somewhere at last. I was spending nights in the tent crying myself to sleep scared that I'd never get out of this problem, I just couldn't see the light at the end of the tunnel, and then it appeared.

Ben and Nadia both did OK at school, Ben didn't do any work for his A Levels and passed them all and Nadia did well in GCSE's but moved to a college to do her A Levels because the schools wouldn't let her do the subjects she wanted. Their grades were never my concern, all I ever wanted was for them to be happy. On their reports teachers always commented on their kindness, it was worth so much more to me than any grade, SO much more.

We couldn't move into the cottage until mid-November and the temperature was about to drop drastically, I was already waking up with everything very damp. Mum had kicked Nadia out, they never really got on because Nadia was so close to me and Mum hated that. When Mum had told Nadia to unload the dishwasher Nadia replied, "you wouldn't ask Ben to do that," which was true, she wouldn't but it riled Mum, as usual, it didn't take much. I'd seen this recently when speaking to her about something else, she lost her temper very quickly and I realised she had the anger problem, probably not me at all. So she'd kicked Nadia out and she was living with Alex and Julie, thank goodness for Julie.

I had to beg Mum to let me stay, if I ever wanted anything Dad would always want to give it to me but I always had to ask Mum. We had a moving date in two weeks or so and reluctantly she agreed to let me stay. I moved in and all seemed OK, treading on eggshells for two weeks, I could just about manage that. Dad loved me being there. Mum did blow one day though, as usual, during another heated exchange over what, I can't remember, she screamed, "we're all alright, it's just you, you're the problem". I kept very quiet.

A week or so later Mum was late coming home and we had no idea why. She arrived home in floods of tears and curled up like a child in her chair. Dad and I were like, "what's wrong? What on earth has happened? What's going on?" she sobbed, like a baby and said, "well if you really, really must know," barely able to get her breathe at all, "if you really must know, it's you Nic". Dad and I looked at each other perplexed, Ben's head dropped. She continued to sob. I got up from my chair, walked over to her and said, "that's it isn't it, this is about **your** jealousy of **his** love for me," pointing at Dad. The penny had dropped, it was crystal clear, at last, my whole life, Mum, Claire and Kerry had all been jealous of Dad's love for me and you can't help being the first born.

DREAM HOME

On November 18th we moved to our beautiful cottage, we're still there, for as long as possible, we all absolutely love it.

I was desperate to get some money for Christmas and so threw the towel in and applied for a housekeeping job that was advertised in the village. It was the Nanny who was recruiting, the owners didn't get involved. I got the job, just down the hill from me in a beautiful barn conversion and I reluctantly loved it, being a cleaner after earning £175kpa isn't an easy comedown. The Nanny left and another arrived which was usual, staff turnover was high. I liked the owner. He wasn't well, had suffered a stroke and heart attack at the same time, so walked with a stick and got confused about some things when speaking but we got along well. One day he text me two or three times, he did often, if he couldn't find stuff, and he put XXX at the end of each one. I didn't know what to do so asked for advice from fellowship friends who all said, "ignore it and carry on as usual", so I ignored it, I replied to his question but kept it very professional with no XXX. When I went in on Monday he couldn't look at me and it was downhill from thereon.

His twenty-five-year younger partner had previously been the mistress who he'd fathered twins with. That's a bit of joke really isn't it, these wealthy people don't have sex to get pregnant they have what they want implanted. My friend said when I got this text, "there's a vacancy, he wants it filled". So after a while I had to leave, it became intolerable, we no longer got on and at every opportunity he'd be angry. Seemed to me he wanted to control me, like the other wealthy people I'd worked for, they think they own you.

I was taking the ACOA meeting for a while and in my gut I knew The Predator would turn up, and he did, I'd mentioned it to a friend and when he turned up she was flabbergasted. Every week that he turned up my heart would pound, it was just daft, but he didn't stay around for long, thank goodness, and I wasn't leaving this meeting because of him, I had to learn to deal with it, it's just a ridiculous love addiction fantasy again, that old chestnut.

I decided to try SAA because this love addiction fantasy was a problem. In Bristol SLAA was very female and I really couldn't get on with it, SAA was predominantly male so I hoped it might be better for me. I started going to meetings and began getting loads of 'no caller id' calls with no one on the end of the line. I got about thirty in a week, then I realised it was Perfect, it was his way of trying to bully me in to not going, but it was my recovery, not his so I continued to go. I did pluck up the courage to go to a meeting that he went to, but he didn't show up so all was OK. I had a panic attack when I got there, dry mouth and trembling with fear, I'd never experienced that before, it really wasn't nice. I suppose being honest, I went to annoy him, he'd stood me up and cancelled so many times I wanted to rattle his cage back, it worked a treat however sick the behaviour was. I apologise, here and now unreservedly, but life is a lesson and I'm always learning, still, as Robert Palmer said '*revenge to honest men isn't sweet*'. I also worked out at this time that although I was besotted with him and sang his praises often, he actually suffered with premature ejaculation. He'd spend ages down there whenever we met and then it would all be over in seconds, he always preferred quick meets in lay-bys and car parks and I slowly realised why. We've not conversed since I mentioned it.

I took up yoga which I now love, tried it before and didn't like it, but I liked this teacher, and have loved it ever since and I was still swimming most days too. When I had an MOT at my surgery around my fifty-fifth I had a resting pulse rate of forty-five which was really good, life was good, I was beginning to get well and like myself, at last.

After yoga on a Friday I could make it to a meeting in Bath which I liked, it had a bit of meditation to begin. Then The Predator turned up. I ignored it and made polite conversation but every time we spoke he was SO nervous, it became ridiculous. His hand would tremble unbelievably, his head would tip slightly back and his eyelids would flutter, like he did when he'd turned up my other small meeting after I blocked him, so I stopped going to the meeting. Absolutely ridiculous but it's not good for me, makes my heart pound, I just don't want or need that, I knew I would become love and fantasy addicted again, time to get out.

I kept going to other local meetings for a while but eventually I tired of it. I'm a puritan, no doubt that comes from my mother yelling at me "why don't you ever get anything right", so I always have to do everything as right as I possibly can so putting down the alcohol was the first step, although the over spending and working had already been curtailed by the recession.

Most people are happy just to be free of alcohol in the fellowship, I can't run with that, I have too many other things that cause me as much harm and I needed to address them. In AA they say 'if you keep going to the barbers you'll get your hair cut', ie don't go to the pub, you'll drink. Being around people with eating disorders, love and sex addictions, co-dependency issues isn't good for me either, just like being amongst heavy drinkers, I wouldn't want to be there so I don't go.

I'd taken another part time cleaning job in the village so that kept me going but it didn't, I was borrowing money off of the children constantly, they earned more than me. I took another cleaning job up to Christmas but hated it. By the end of March I'd had enough and signed on, first time in many, many years. Pretty quickly I got a month's credit control work with an agency that provided concierge staff, cleaners and the like, I'm not good with their rhetoric anyway so I didn't stay.

I was in touch with the 6'+ red-haired guy from AA, he'd called and asked me for a drink some months earlier which I went for, and then he had to rush off which I had to accept disappointingly. Later I got a text saying he had to go because he felt something and didn't want to act on it, I wasn't sure what he meant but hoped. We continued to message each other and rarely bumped into each other but he was always very happy to see me when we did, and the texts slowly turned to sexting. This went on for a while and I, foolishly, was flattered. He was still married with two children and I was still desperate.

He arranged to meet me in a lay by and it was a snog in his car which culminated in a blow job, but it didn't get very hard, most odd, he said it wasn't usually like that. We then arranged to meet a few more times, he had me driving miles and turning up here and there and he never showed "my wife has fallen asleep with her head on my lap," was one of the excuses I remember. Eventually he came to my house one Sunday afternoon, he's the only man who ever has. I spring cleaned the whole place and dug the garden, whatever for I really don't know, but aren't I trying to impress him, trying to say "look at this lovely home I have, come and share it with me", how stupid am I. After a snog we raced upstairs and got naked and did some more amorous kissing and he did the usual down there while I moaned and groaned a bit and then I went to get on top and it wasn't hard, again. He just couldn't get it hard. He started to make the usual excuses, I'm tired, it's not usually like this, I've never had this problem before, I just couldn't believe it, he's had hundreds of women, is prolific on sex dating sites and yet he can't get it up? Maybe that's it, maybe it's what we can't have that we're addicted to, like I'm addicted to love because I've never had it, so I crave it? I remembered later though he'd told me that many years ago, whilst off his face at a party an older man had had sex with him and he'd liked it, maybe he's gay and can't come to terms with it, who knows? He clearly doesn't.

The guy I said, "I'm going to have you," to at my neighbours fortieth I met out on another night. We went back to his friends, I thought for a threesome but found them half naked stroking and caressing each other when I resurfaced from drunken oblivion. I don't think these women don't know I just think they turn a blind eye because they're happy with their children and life and it all plays along nicely thank you very much, until the shit hits the fan. It happened to a local clergyman, it all comes out in the wash, or death.

Another gay man I know who is on Grinder (Tinder for gay men, just in case you didn't know because I didn't) insists that the vast majority, in fact almost all, of the meets he has are with married guys with kids. The biggest selling sex toy currently is a strap on dildo, being bought by straight couples. I'm not sure I agree with the born gay stance either. I believe homosexuality comes from the same childhood trauma and family dysfunction as alcoholism and all other addictions and most probably many diseases and illnesses, including I'm sure, bi-polar and anxiety. We each deal with this stuff differently as we all experience it differently and so it manifests itself as diversely too. The only reason homosexuality is legal is because it's perpetrated by the wealthy elite who can change the law to suit themselves, and did, they experience this stuff the same as us it can just look prettier with money thrown at it.

In aggravation I did regress and met with the professional guy I knew in a lay-by one cold dark night with nothing on but a mac. A snog and grope ensued but guess what, he couldn't get it up! Is that why he's on a sex site, because he can't? Or is it me? I don't think so. I'm seriously wondering if a lot of the men that are addicted to sex and sex sites, and there are many, very, very many, actually can't perform. I wonder if it's a huge problem that isn't discussed because it's too shaming.

I went to see the psychic for some hope that things might get better. Amongst other stuff she told me they would, she was no longer telling me to live for now I noticed which she'd always said previously. She said someone was going to get very, very thirsty and needed to see a doctor urgently, so I kept saying to Nad and Ben "is nanny thirsty? she needs to see the doctor if she is, she might be diabetic". And someone was going to have a cycling accident so I kept warning my neighbour to be careful, she cycled to work daily. And someone had to stay with the crowd and not wander off, so every time the children went out "make sure you stay with your friends, don't wander off alone". And the usual that I've been told many times "you're emigrating to Australia". I'm bored of that one, been told it a few times in the last four or five years and I can only conclude that I would go back there for Simon, no other reason but it kept the fantasy alive, I'd forgotten that I wasn't interested last time we met.

In Aldi recently I bumped into Simon's niece and asked if he was coming over for his big birthday soon thinking that must be it, we'll meet up and the fantasy would conclude. She looked at me with sadness in her eyes and said that a few years ago he was out on his own on a bike ride, in the middle of nowhere and fell off, he dehydrated and later died in hospital. I had to walk away, I was shocked, my heart broke and the tears fell. My fantasy of returning to Australia to live the rest of my life with him was crushed and he was dead. I couldn't believe it. I kept crying for a week or so, sad, so very, very sad. I still can't see why I'd emigrate to Australia though, couldn't afford to for a start.

I was sending my CV for loads of jobs but they were all with agencies, I hate agencies, they get a contract and pay the workers as little as possible. I absolutely hate them and they won't entertain anyone over fifty in my experience either.

Eventually an employer posted a credit control position and I got the job, I've been there a while now. I love the job, but think I prefer working from home where I can just get on with it. I'm perhaps realising I'm best alone, but in a position where I have contact with a lot of people.

THE LAST KISS

Mum was eighty in November and having a tea party at a local hotel with a hundred or so guests which I wasn't invited to, as usual, it's still all my fault. Ben and Nadia had to go so I wanted something to do and had a tiny 'fuck it' moment, they are very rare now though, less than bi-annually, I know the consequences too well. So I contacted Sam, who I've not seen in nine years but I knew he lived near and was hopefully single, sometimes he is, I always put a proviso on these contacts, "if you aren't single I apologise". This was months before, I asked if he were free, didn't expect a reply but got one and so on this afternoon I went to his to play hide the sausage. I really don't want to go to my grave not knowing the name of the last man I had sex with. It was odd really, I'd not seen him in nine years, since just after my boob job and yet it felt very normal, like nothing had happened in between but of course it had. I was divorced now and sober, not really that different but he got the one to one version of this story which took a while, in not quite such explicit detail though. We do get on, well I think we do, very well, but hide the sausage was not to be, he'd played rugby the day before and was hobbling like an older man sadly. Four hours flew by and then he had to go and meet friends so it was one very gorgeous snog and that was it. He said to "get in touch," "come over," "let's go out for coffee or a drink", at which point I was slightly confused, why would we do that? What for? so I did say "you can't say that, I'll be here tomorrow", I had just confessed to being a massive love addict and this was fuel for the fire.

A week or so went by and he didn't contact me so I messaged him and he replied each time quite promptly but was always busy, then he said weekdays were better so I said "OK I'm free Monday, Wednesday or Friday," and I've not heard from him since regrettably. I've always really liked him but maybe he's a jealous or tight man and the universe is keeping me safe, that's what I chose to believe anyway, how else can I cope with the rejection? By eating a mountain of food and throwing up? By drinking myself to a stupor? By getting on a sex site and fucking some other random? By going on a spending spree that I can't afford? The things I do to quell how I feel are now more sombre, I walk the dog, I do yoga, I swim vigorously, I call someone though I don't really have friends, I'd rather be alone, bar with Ben and Nadia. People hurt, hence my oldest best friends being food, love addiction or fantasy, and alcohol.

No doubt Sam just isn't interested, I suppose I'm a bit of a handful and heaven forbid if any of these men read this, I'll never see them again and that's probably exactly how it's meant to be.

Weeks later I called Brad as he knows Sam and I asked him what was wrong with me that he never wanted me as a girlfriend, what did I do wrong? To which he replied, "Nic it's not you, men are just insecure pricks and I had loads of women around that time I met you, I was going through a difficult phase". His brother had died and he had massive guilt about not protecting him from the man up the road but, of course, the shame of it means they never talked about it, which is why the perpetrators get away with it.

THIS WONDERFUL LIFE

I think religion was created to control the poor, the uneducated and women. Men realised that women have it all and so had to control them.

You can also see on any nature programme how it's the female that does all the work, brings up the children, cooks, washes and cleans while the man lounges around with his mates. So long as they're fed and watered and have a blow job on Sundays they're generally happy it seems. Women build nests, men live in them, we're put on this earth to look after them and they know it.

Some bloke with a small dick wrote the bit in that book about monogamy and although having one partner is preferable, comforting, reassuring and secure and I think we all like that, we are now a society of serial monogamists. The days of twenty years and more together are going, almost gone, we have relationships for approximately thirteen years apparently, seems about right, and then we're on to the next one, if we can find them. The days are numbered for that book to survive though too, we are in the age of Pisces, we have about one hundred or so years to go and we'll move into the age of Aries and then religion will be no more. Amen to that! I never was any good with believing a man, let alone a blonde haired, blue eyed one on a cloud was running this wonderful show.

I realise now I was very '*my way or the highway*' in my thinking, I wonder if my putting up the chairs at primary school was showing this fear and controlling behaviour? Maybe that's wrong, I'm not actually 100% sure, maybe it's just that women have a problem with women. That seems a real possibility. Why have viewing figures for Dr Who plummeted since she became female? I wonder if we're like lionesses after our lion and we will fight to get what we want, it's not the men that do the fighting, you only have to watch The Apprentice to see that play out, I don't watch it anymore for that exact reason, or maybe that's just the way the producers want it to be seen. I don't want to believe it but in my experience I can't find evidence to the contrary.

My friend is doing a PHD in why women don't stay in the media industry. Managerially it's dominated by men, the women leave, yet at Uni level 80% of students are female. Marie, my nurse friend of years back said similarly that when men were nurses they were usually not very good (she said they were rubbish) so they were promoted to get them off the floor. And there are many industries where women do the work and men manage them, why? I wonder if it's just that we, as women, take ten years or more off for children? I just don't get it really, why men are in charge when women do the work, is it just a physical strength thing? Or maybe we just aren't so interested in being in charge, we value what matters, love, and raising children or looking after each other. Men can keep the winning, it's part of the disease of more.

The fellowship is just the newest church really, supposedly without God. Members quote that the word *alcohol* (or whatever other addiction is pertinent to that particular fellowship) is 'only in the steps once'. The word God or Higher Power is in the steps six times though. It is, and was, Christian to begin. Then they realised that excluded a lot of people so amended it, a bit like the bible, they tweaked it as they went along but it's remained the same for a while now, has been around eighty plus years and is thriving, thank goodness. It can help tremendously, in fact after rehab I felt so clean, like all the crap in my emotional cupboards had been dealt with I'd highly recommend it to anyone, in fact everyone. Not rehab necessarily, just time with people who love and care for you unreservedly, without judgement and you will find them there.

I'm not sure if it'll survive too much longer unless they remove the God/Higher Power thing. That said, I did have to find a belief in something to get well, otherwise I'd continue to believe what my Mother had taught me and stay sick. So slowly through loads of meetings, talking, listening and being around people on a similar journey I began to realise she wasn't right, she's sick, anyone that's cruel is sick, fighting their own battles no doubt, but that's their journey not mine. I can only change me. 'If you want to make the world a better place take a look at yourself and make a change' comes to mind. I realised that this universe created me. I came through my Mother and Father, of all those sperm in my Dad around Christmas 1961 this one got through, this one was meant to be, I am meant to be happy, healthy and loved, as we all are.

The fellowships are exactly that, eye to eye contact, love and support. I wish there were a fellowship called JLS, 'just love and support'. We are all fighting our own battles that no one knows about, though I feel you know mine now and I hope it's been interesting to say the least, if you got this far it can't not have been I suppose.

I am concerned I'll be ostracised and vilified for speaking about the fellowship because they're very fond of 'who you see here, what you hear here, when you leave here let it stay here' and then in the next breath they'll tell you 'it's secrets that keep you sick'. Honesty is always best, truth is always best but what I think I've come to realise is that there is no truth and I say that because there are ten thousand shades of black and ten thousand shades of white and I'd chose that one and you'd chose another. Neither of us is right, or wrong, but our journey in life gives us different ideas of what is right and wrong, black and white, rich and poor, old and young, happy and sad, the list is endless. Like flowers and weeds, you'll like that one, I'll like another. We are like snowflakes, we're all the same but we're all different.

I was raised by a man who adored me but abandoned me and left me with a mother who was jealous of that love and me. I still feel some women are jealous of me, I'm so aware of it I stay away from them, I just don't get what they're jealous of. The trouble is I stay away from men too. That's just my life. I like being alone, bar Ben and Nadia, people hurt. But without knowing sad I wouldn't know happy.

Part of the journey in the fellowship is acknowledging that our parents 'did the best they could with what they had', so that we don't blame them. I'm not good with that especially when my mother continues to blame me, to this day. On the few rare occasions that I've tried to have a relationship with her by going back in slowly, building up my time with her in ten minute increments she's always brought out the 'well we're alright it's just you' card within thirty minutes.

I can say now I love myself, I accept myself just the way I am, I'm OK, not better than anyone and not worse, I'm me and that's enough. Maybe I'm not thick, maybe I'm no longer fat and maybe I never was ugly. I still don't have boyfriends, don't suppose I ever will but I'm not unlovable, my children love me and I them, more than words will ever be able to say. I chose to not have relationships with those who still blame and persecute me because I have that choice and it keeps me safe and well. I was quite simply an unloved, neglected and rejected child.

I wonder if I would have got to this happy place without AA, I think not. When I meet people who haven't experienced 'The Programme' I wish they had. I wish they'd just give it a go, for a while, probably at ACOA though, because it's never about what we do, it's always why we do it. We've all got this stuff in varying degrees, we all have an Achilles heel and need a space where we can be totally and completely honest and loved and accepted without judgement for who we are. There are as many ways to work the programme as there are people in it, take what you need and leave the rest.

In February 2020 while I was finishing writing this and my ego got a hold I thought to myself, "what's the best thing that could come of this and in my mind I thought maybe sitting on the sofa opposite Phil and Holly for a minute or two would be good". My next thought was, "no they're too perfect, they're the problem, we all think that's how our lives should be, Barbie and Ken, Kate and Will, it all looks so perfect, I'd rather sit with Kathy Burke and be real". A few days later Philip came out on TV.

I think of that lovely scene in Titanic when Kate and Leonardo are dancing on tables downstairs and the posh are having tea upstairs, I'd rather be downstairs any day with a karaoke and disco. I just want to be happy and that doesn't come with the disease of more which I feel those upstairs are completely consumed by. Being grateful for what I have right here and now is crucial. Realising and understanding that there is nothing I can buy that will fix me, I am well as I am. Loving myself just as I am, despite all this that has gone before is a monumental accomplishment in my eyes and has brought peace and contentment, writing this has contributed to that which amazes me. I might not being saying that if there's a backlash from it. We'll see. This too shall pass.

I heard or read years ago there are four things needed for contentment

1) Something to love
2) Something to be loved by
3) Enough money for our needs not necessarily our wants
4) A purpose

I wonder if something to look forward to could be added to that list but maybe *a purpose* encompasses that.

Addiction is a disease of isolation, of not belonging, of feeling alone, believing that no one else would understand or get you. I believe we are all addicts, but some addictions seem healthier than others, like wealth and power they're the ones that can be most devastating to humankind and the planet and yet these people have the disease of more beyond our comprehension. A businessman is so revered and yet he it seems to me he sells at a profit, for his own greed and wealth. The disease of more, the corroboration of which is none so more affirmed than in a businessman, or woman, a crook in reality. If we invent, create or find something that is of such value to mankind is it not better to give it freely?

Marriage can be a love addiction and unhealthy, people who can't live without each other or a partner, that's unhealthy, if you can't live without someone then you have a problem, you're addicted to that person. Even prescribed drugs, pharmaceutical companies create customers, rarely cures. Doctors can be legal drug dealers.

A daily reprieve only comes from self-awareness and acceptance, and love of self and isn't that the hardest one, to love thyself? Especially when we've been given crap by other sick people that as children we think is right because after all they are teaching us aren't they? They are our lead, our teachers, our way in this world so we have to believe them don't we? No one would ever dare question a teacher or of course their mother. A mother is a child's most influential teacher, if they're around and whether they're right or not, as a child we'll believe them.

Whenever I brought up the pain from childhood with my parents or siblings they'd complain, "why do you keep bringing that up, it was fifty years ago," but it never leaves, ever, it's my wiring and will never change, ever, I can deal with it better now though, and that's much easier without them in my life sadly. And Mum and Claire were only to cruel to me that I know of, I suppose once they'd found someone that would take the blame they just kept giving it.

I struggle to believe there is mental illness. It seems to me there is only childhood trauma and family dysfunction. Nadia recently did Psychology A level and asked various stuff along the way. My understanding is that while they were exploring addiction they realised it came from childhood trauma and dysfunction. When they told the poor they accepted that they might be responsible for their child's problems, but when they told the middle classes they weren't having any of it and so the term *'mental illness'* was created to alleviate their burden. Schizophrenia, in my experience, I've only known three people diagnosed, is due to medication, excessive medication, not a natural state at all, in my experience.

We are all victims of victims, all our Grandfathers or Great Grandfathers have served in wars and seen such atrocities. If they return at all they return with so many scars and afflictions they have no chance of leading a sane existence and we inherit the remnants of those experiences and we all deal with these terrors differently.

I always thought my problem was my weight, if I could be slim all would be perfect. It's not that at all, in losing weight all I'm doing is putting down the drug, the medicine I've learned to use over many, many, many years, that's why diet's don't work, it's not about food. Putting that drug down leaves me with my thoughts and feelings which all go back to my childhood trauma and family dysfunction, everything in my life comes from that time, those very young years, all my programming comes from that experience. I've had to heal those wounds. I'm not sure I'm done, I don't suppose I ever will be. Those wounds are why I'm better off away from my parents and siblings, and with Nadia and Ben and maybe a few others, very few and I like it this way, life is good, at last.

Therapy helped along the way, it helped me to understand where I came from, with understanding I can accept, with acceptance I can forgive, with forgiveness I can move on and change. Therapists, in all their many, many guises, I feel are often actually in it for themselves, all really trying to work out what's wrong with them, or maybe that's just my experience of some of them. I think we study this stuff to help ourselves ultimately, not others. Therapists, psychologists, psychotherapists and counsellors are just blank walls to talk to, all the answers are in you but you need someone to talk them to or will probably think you are mad trying to work it out. I think ACOA is better than therapy because no one has any authority, we are co-travellers, we work it out ourselves as we go, by talking about it openly with people who love and care for us and we have the best big red book. And in my experience what works one time or for a while, might not work later as we grow and move forward, our lives are forever evolving as are the people we need in them to help us move on. The only person that knows you though is you.

As human beings we are eternally hopeful, after all we're born knowing we're going to die and we're forever trying to make the best of this journey of life.

I've discovered that when I think I know something I stop learning, yet when I acknowledge that I don't know something I learn so much because my heart and mind are open to new ideas and I keep looking for the answer and solution and so am continually learning during that process.

I will always have a food problem to battle with I'm sure but it's getting better slowly. I try to eat very little sugar or flour and still struggle with the masses of cakes at work consuming more than anyone else when they're around. I've put a deep black box out for them so I don't have to see them when I walk past as I still want to eat the whole packet of biscuits or whole large chocolate bar or even the whole cake if there is one sometimes. It's only very recently I've walked past the stuff in Aldi thinking, "it won't fix me, leave it alone".

I need exercise so I chose to park my car two miles from work and walk for an hour, two miles there and back daily. I swim for half an hour each day I'm at work too. Importantly I'm usually with people all day, even though my head tells me I want to be alone. I think if I were to work from home for too long I'd become depressed. I did think isolation catapults me into misery and self-loathing but three weeks into COVID-19 and I'm really good, loving being home but I do have my children here and Eric. If the children weren't here it might be different.

I don't earn anywhere near what I used to but I earn enough to get by. I no longer spend like a lunatic to fix myself, I do love to go away and out with Nadia and Ben though so that's our treat if I have any excess funds. Being grateful for what I have is paramount to my wellbeing. Loving what I have, my children, and Eric, my walk to work, my swim, bit of yoga, my health, life is good, really good, at last, I no longer think, "if I had that... life would be good". Life is good now, right now.

I do wonder if my children will leave and loathe me as much as I do my mother, and that's putting it mildly, I sincerely hope not but I can't be sure. What I do know is there isn't a day in their lives when I haven't looked at them and said, "I love you," and put my arms around them and kissed them and I just hope that my theory of, "love is always the answer," is right, perhaps I'll know in another forty years or so. I'll let you know.

I've realised on writing this how we spent hours in pubs with Ben and Nadia, following my parents path. I apologise to Ben and Nadia a lot, and they often and usually reply, "it wasn't bad Mum, promise". I also realise that I've pushed men away or ran on the few occasions they wanted 'in'. But when we acknowledge we have a problem we're half way to solving it, here's hoping. As my window cleaner friend says, "I only want someone in my life if they make me happi...er".

I applied to go on 'The Chase' the other day and realised I'd done this video for them so thought why not apply to 'First Dates' too so I did. They called on Monday surprisingly. And then that fear engulfs me, what if someone actually liked me? They won't if they really know me surely? But maybe that's not true, the producer interviewing me said I reminded him of Julie Walters which is just lovely. And I've been likened to Glenn Close often, although she usually plays a baddie. More recently my daughters friends said I look like Gillian Anderson! Not so ugly after all.

Life is for living, not thinking about, do no harm and so long as the sky blue, grass green and birds singing all will be well.

Love is always the answer.

My children and Eric

A WORD ON FOOD

Sugar is a drug, it has no nutritional value whatsoever, and calories aren't nutrition, they're fuel, it does 8/10 things heroin and cocaine do to the brain. . I'm not talking about the sugar in whole fruits and vegetables, that's ok, providing it's in the **whole** fruit or vegetable because that has fibre in it. Flour is sugar, the same, refined carbohydrate, no nutritional value. Wholemeal flour is a bit better, anything with fibre in makes us poo better so wholemeal isn't so bad, but the white stuff just makes us fat, as does sugar but it's a drug and most are very addicted to it. In the fifties they were telling us smoking was good for us! Now sugar is ok, sugar (flour is refined sugar/carbohydrate) is the new smoking, they inject it to find cancer because it feeds it, simplistic but true, it causes inflammation, arthritis and dementia along with obesity which can lead to strokes and heart attacks, and cancer. All those 'no calorie' sugar substitutes are equally bad, if not worse than sugar, our brains don't know the difference.

I trained with a large weight loss company a couple of years ago and left because they promote masses of processed foods with loads of sugar in. Read 'Pure White and Deadly' by John Yudkin if you want the science.

Fat does not make you fat, Ancel Keys, the physiologist and 'low-fat' theorist manipulated statistics, if it's low fat it has more sugar, sugar is the demon.

Originally we were running around and killing our food, it was when we began to grow grains and settle in communities that our teeth started to rot and we put on weight, we don't need grains in our diet, but guess what, it makes money so they'll tell us we do.

To lose weight cut sugar and flour from your diet as much as possible it's that simple.

Printed in Poland
by Amazon Fulfillment
Poland Sp. z o.o., Wrocław

58829746R00074